ARCTIC PARADISE

ARCTIC PARADISE

The Paradox of Finnish Happiness

SUSANNA HEISKANEN

ARCTIC PARADISE
The Paradox of Finnish Happiness

ISBN: 978-0-6454739-7-1 Paperback
ISBN: 978-0-6454739-8-8 Hardback
ISBN: 978-0-6454739-9-5 Ebook
ISBN: 978-0-6486155-0-7 Audiobook

Published by The Nordic Mum
Copyright © 2024 Susanna Heiskanen
Susanna Heiskanen asserts her moral rights as identified as the author of this work.

www.thenordicmumbooks.com
Facebook: susannaheiskanenauthor
Instagram: @susannaheiskanenwrites

Previous books:

NORDIC LIFESTYLE
Embrace slow living, cultivate happiness and know when to take off your shoes

CONTENTS

To Jayne, Alison and Felicity.

The world is always a better place after talking with you.

"Happiness is a place between too little and too much."

Finnish proverb

Introduction

The sixth annual World Happiness Report has just been published. As I sit down to write, Finland tops the charts again. I could not be happier for all our Nordic neighbours, every one of us in the top 10. And for good reason. Which brings me to this book. I had a powerful pull to talk about happiness and Finland, perhaps looking at it more critically. While we have mastered happiness, according to the charts and measurements of the World Happiness Report, there are a few notable omissions!

When you talk to Finns about these rankings, they find them amusing. People laugh and shrug their shoulders, ignoring that the world is talking about Finland and Finnish happiness right now. Finns are coy that we live in a pretty awesome place called *Suomi* in our language, a place that is happy and where people are content. Finns are also modest. Our reaction to the news is not euphoria or celebration as you might expect. Finns take life as it comes.

I wanted to understand what makes Finland the happiest country in the world. What makes us so happy that there are tons of articles written about it? There are blogs, podcasts and even documentaries (*Why Finland and Denmark are Happier than the US*) made about Finnish people and how happy we are. Why are people obsessed with Finnish happiness? Why does Finland's happiness come as a surprise? And most of all, is it really as rosy as the reports will have us believe?

Along with a look at the landscape, I wanted to give some practical examples and takeaway tips on how the theory can and does translate into reality. How can *you* have some of this Finnish happiness in *your* life? How can you – or anyone – affect your own happiness? What practical actions can you take to be happier in life? What tools are out there? Or is it more about an internal mindset?

When looking at happiness, here's what the 2023 World Happiness Report was measuring. They explored happiness around the world and what this would look like in different countries.

They included the following six key factors:

- Income

- Health

- Having someone to count on

- Having a sense of freedom to make key life decisions

- Generosity

- Absence of corruption

This, of course, is not an exhaustive list of what happiness is. It does not measure mindset, not that I think mindset can even be measured accurately. It also does not look at the individual level, more focused on happiness *as a society*.

I hope this book gives you a glimpse of happiness in Finland. I hope you take away some practical tips of what to add, change or include in your daily life to be happier, even if you do not live in Finland, but want to introduce some of these Finnish ways into your life. Perhaps you want to travel to Finland to experience Arctic Paradise for yourself. Or perhaps you are a Finnophile and just cannot get enough *sisu* and all good things Made in Finland.

So that you have a balanced view, I will also cover the not-so-pleasant side of Finnish society. Why does Finland still have work to do? Issues like racism, far-right politics, mental health issues and alcohol use remind us that there is a dark side to the world's narrow view of our Arctic Paradise. There is a less sunny side of Finnish society, which needs to be mentioned and cannot be ignored if we are to truly investigate happiness.

Whatever the reason, I am happy you are here. Let's dive in and see what makes Finland the happiest place on earth.

What a Finn in Australia has to say about Finland!

First, I want to tell you about my journey from Finland to Australia and how this book came into being. I started writing a different book than the one you are reading right now. After my first book *Nordic Lifestyle: Embrace Slow Living, Cultivate Happiness and Know When To Take Off Your Shoes,* I wrote the beginnings of another book about Nordic lifestyle, culture and history with some self-reflections. It was like a Volume 2 of my *Nordic Lifestyle* book.

I was 30,000 words deep when I realised, I was stuck. I had already covered much of what I had to say. Perhaps it was a sign, but when my computer was playing up one day and I hadn't saved the draft (in two or three places like I do now), I lost the book.

Writing my first book *Nordic Lifestyle* had been such an easy task, because I had the podcast Nordic Mum covering some of the same topic. Here I was now with no words, feeling like my creative well had run dry. I know it was not really a sign I should give up, but I felt downtrodden and beaten by the whole process. I took some time off and gathered my thoughts.

It seemed like a good idea that all my books share some connection to 'Nordicness' within them, but how to make it happen without overly repeating myself? Well, I was not sure, but I brainstormed what would be useful for you, the reader, what you would enjoy, and what knowledge I could share with you.

This book came from that thinking process. Seeing myself become happy and knowing what happiness means to me, I set out to write about what the culture was like in Finland and how it compared to here in Australia.

Why Australia?

To be honest, it had been my wish for as long as I can remember – to experience Australia and to live here. I had never been to Australia when I arrived here in January 2008, but I had dreamed about seeing it. The company I worked for had conveniently booked me into accommodation in Circular Quay. No complaints from me! I walked around Sydney Harbour, taking it all in, thinking, *'Wow! This is my new home'.*

Still, I felt like an intruder, but let's take a step back to how I ended up wandering around Circular Quay that January after four months in Auckland.

My first memories of Australia were seeing Summer Bay on the TV show *Home and Away* and watching *Neighbours* on the telly back in Finland. I always thought what a fascinating place it would be to live and hoped to travel there one day. Then when I moved to London in my early 20s, still fascinated by all things 'down under', I met my best friend, who is Australian. I loved asking her about the culture, customs, food and lifestyle. It was really eye-opening for me coming from a smallish town in rural Finland and never having been anywhere really.

In London, I embraced the different cultures that I came across, but the thought of moving again was already in the back of my mind. Once in London, I worked and dreamed about moving to Australia. The thought never really left my head, but I was not sure how to do it. *'What do I need to do to get there?'* I buried the thought for a while and just enjoyed life in London, travelling and seeing as much of the UK as I could with my then-boyfriend (now-husband).

I recall looking into the visa process and being put off by the complicated system and everything I was required to do to apply and get there. One option was a skilled visa or business-sponsored visa. I was studying for my degree in London for that reason. The Australian visa I had looked at stated I would need a degree. Studying and working at the same time are not for the fainthearted and I took a few times to pass my exams, while stressing about the fact I had full-time work. In the end, work gave me a day off per week to study and that made the process more manageable. Given I was considering resigning, my company was very accommodating to give me time off to study!

At the end of 2006, I started the long process of getting myself to Australia. I negotiated a move with my employer, a global medical and security assistance company with offices around the world. I was happy to go into any position, but

I was told that a transfer had to be to a similar role as I was doing at the time, which was assistant manager for their alarm centre.

At the end of 2007, I was told that I could move, but I would have to go to Auckland, New Zealand for a few months first. New Zealand had been on my bucket list ever since the *Lord of the Rings* movies hit cinemas a few years before and I was hooked. I wanted to see these glorious places that I had only seen in the movies for myself. I loved my time in New Zealand. I loved everything about the slow pace of life, the smiley happy people and the hospitable feeling that people were genuinely interested in you.

After four months in Auckland, I did not want to leave. I was even offered an opportunity to stay and I know I would have been happy there. While these two countries are similar for a Finn, they are also different, so I felt torn. I thought I might have better opportunities in Australia and that I would be able to advance in my career and go places. That was my only real reason to move to Australia, at that time, but I had also committed to Sydney. So, finally, I was on my way in January of 2008.

When I arrived, it felt surreal. I recall feeling happy but wondering how things really worked! One of the most bizarre feelings was being in a country that was a continent. It was so huge that you could not really get your head around how it takes a day to fly from one end to the other. The second thing I remember occurring to me was how it was possible that everyone spoke English here. We were on the other side of the world from the UK, but New Zealand and Australia were English-speaking countries.

Here I was, fresh from the UK via New Zealand and ready to work my butt off to stay in this glorious country. I was struck by how different the nature was; all the plants looked nothing like those in Finland or the UK. The birds were loud and colourful. The animals looked strange. I was expecting to see kangaroos everywhere, but my taxi driver from the airport burst my bubble, laughing at my suggestion! I could not have imagined how different the scenary was even if I tried. But in a good way! I did stay, after all.

Here I am, 20-plus years later, now a citizen and able to vote, work and live in this beautiful country that I call home.

Finland

However, my roots are always in Finland and my Finnishness comes out every so often, as my English husband likes to tell me. Particularly when my two sons were born, I thought more and more about who I was and what it meant to have a child while not living in your country of birth. I made connections with other bilingual mothers and immersed myself in Finnish culture through audiobooks, *Finnish School* (for kids outside Finland) and making friends with Finnish parents.

I always identified as a Finn and I have tried to pollinate my kids with lots of Finnish traits like love for salted liquorice (successfully) that my husband abhors. The older they have become, the more they see themselves as three parts: Australian, English and Finnish. To my mother's dismay though, Australia comes first. But as my husband says, if they are good at sports, they have three countries to choose from when they decide who to represent in the Olympics.

What about happiness though? I miss some things that I used to take for granted in Finland. Like everything *just worked*. Let me explain. From the bus or train coming on time, the ticket being purchased and paid for, to the fact that you felt secure if you were on transport or arriving at the station along. You could eat without feeling harassed or unsafe.

When you looked up the next train, a friendly staff member would tell you where to go and how to get to your platform. Each of these steps were easy or required nothing else from you except that you turn up and follow the instructions. Life was simple.

Everything in Finnish society is built with the aim of making your life easier. I recall watching in awe when Sanna Marin was chosen as the next prime minister of Finland at the age of 34 back in December 2019. Overnight, Finland was everywhere in the news. Her comments at the World Economic Forum echo what many people think about Finland:

"I feel that the American Dream can be achieved best in the Nordic countries, where every child, no matter their background or the background of their families, can become anything."

She is an example of this – coming from a rainbow family, from an average suburb of Tampere, her hometown.

This, to me, is one of the core reasons why Finland is a content country, where people are happier than perhaps the average person in the world. You do not need to make an *effort* to be happy when your surrounding society takes care of you and your needs.

Inevitably, I compare Australia to Finland. I know I shouldn't! These are two different countries with two very different societies. Australia being very diverse though isolated geographically and Finland being less diverse but being a crossroads between Europe and Russia. In Australia, the year-round sunshine makes people smile more than average Finn and Australians come across as more grounded and 'no worries' type of people. As I will explore, Finns display their happiness through their actions more so than smiling. Finns believe, at times, taking *less* action can mean more happiness: such as sitting by a lake, taking in the beautiful nature, smelling the summer.

I wonder what we could borrow from Finland here in Australia to embrace the Arctic Paradise style of happiness. And since both countries have positives that I love, let's see how we can learn from each other.

PART ONE

THE POSITIVES

What is this *paradox* of Finnish happiness?

I wanted to address happiness in two parts: the positives of why Finland is a pretty awesome and content country (in the next few chapters) and then the negatives, the not so happy things (at the end of the book).

I felt that there was a *paradox* in Finnish happiness and that each area of Finnish society needed a chapter on the negatives in their own right. For a balanced view, I wanted to include those areas, not only write about the good things in life. However, feel free to skip those chapters if you feel they are not for you!

We'll start by talking about the Finnish *mindset* and how important it is in making Finland a resilient country to live in.

"Be happy about the things you have and not be sad about the things you don't have. Because a fact of life is that you can't have everything, no matter what you do. Learn to appreciate what you have in your life. Don't worry about the things you didn't get."

Anonymous

CHAPTER 1

The Finnish Mindset

Happiness is often associated with external factors such as material possessions, social status or life events. However, research has shown that happiness is also strongly related to mindset and the way that we perceive and interpret the world around us. In fact, many experts believe that our mindset is one of the most important factors in determining our overall happiness and well-being.

Happiness is about mindset not about your bank balance or worldly possessions. As a Finn, I believe we do not need anything more than our mind to be optimistic and happy about life. I would also say that Finns are pretty optimistic people. Optimism refers to the tendency to expect positive outcomes and to view setbacks or challenges as temporary and surmountable. Research by the American Psychological Association shows that optimistic individuals are happier and more resilient than their pessimistic counterparts in work, marriage, health and life in general.

This is because optimism allows individuals to focus on the positives in life, even in the face of adversity, as well as to maintain a sense of hope and possibility. Finns do not allow little things to crush their spirit. They see silver linings everywhere, even when it is dark most of the year in Finland. Finns enjoy the sunlight when we have it, of course, but life continues as normal when it is dark or rainy during the day. You do not hide when it is dark all day. It is just part of the life cycle. Finns, well, they just get on with life.

Mindset also plays a role in our ability to cope with stress and adversity. Individuals with a growth mindset, for example, view challenges as opportunities for learning and developing themselves, rather than as threats or setbacks. This mindset helps individuals stay motivated and resilient in the face of difficulty and retain a sense of hope and possibility. Much has been written about Finland in wartime and how we have won against the odds many times over. Some say that it is down to our *sisu,* a Finnish concept that I will talk about later

in this book. It's that optimistic attitude that Finns show – not giving up, believing in yourself and your abilities to get through when you're in a tight spot.

Think back to a time in your life when you were the happiest you have been. The almost overwhelming feeling of happiness, such as the day you fell in love, married your sweetheart or gave birth to your baby. A moment when you felt invincible and nothing could hurt or harm you. A moment you want to carry with you always and know will last forever. That is the real happiness that the Finnish mindset embraces.

A positive mindset can also affect our relationships with others. In Finland, people with a positive mindset are more open to feedback and collaboration. They may be more willing to compromise and communicate effectively in relationships. This can lead to more feelings of connection and satisfaction with others, which can contribute to greater happiness and well-being. I see this more with younger generations that are

perhaps able to share their feelings and communicate better with each other.

I believe a positive mindset plays a critical role in determining our level of happiness and well-being. By cultivating an optimistic, grateful and growth-oriented mindset, individuals can *learn* to focus on the positives in life, cope more effectively with stress and adversity, and build more fulfilling relationships with others. This Finnish mindset, being content and open for growth, is one of the key factors of lasting happiness. And yes, it is free to practice wherever you are!

Happiness research looks at how people's mental health and physical well-being are connected and looked after. The World Happiness Report, for example, found that more money should be allocated to mental health therapies, which are shown to support mental well-being generally. These are more cost-effective for societies in the long run as well. Even more so, providing preventative measures (in the form of health education, information and screening) for mental illness and capturing the onset of illness early are proving cost-effective.

Despite the Finnish mindset, there are issues around how mental health is treated in Finland and it is not all Arctic Paradise, which I will talk about more in later chapters.

Personal freedom

One measure of happiness that the World Happiness Report 2023 includes is that of personal freedom. This is defined *as the ability of individuals to make choices that affect their lives without interference from others*. This measure is based on indicators such as civil liberties, political rights, freedom of expression and freedom of association.

The report finds that personal freedom is strongly associated with happiness and well-being. Countries with high levels of personal freedom have higher levels of happiness and life satisfaction, as well as better social outcomes, such as less corruption, greater gender equality and more trust. One reason for this association may be that personal freedom allows individuals to pursue their own goals and aspirations and to express themselves freely without fear of reprisal. In Finland, this translates to freedom to study, work, travel and live wherever you choose. Individuals have the support of society as a whole to grow and contribute, giving more feelings of autonomy and self-determination, which can contribute to greater happiness and well-being.

In addition, personal freedom can foster higher levels of trust and social cohesion, as individuals are more likely to respect and value the rights and freedoms of others when they themselves are free to make choices and express themselves. In Finland, you are free to make choices about how to live your life. Society is open and welcoming. It allows you to make mistakes and helps you when you need guidance. For example, Finns can access tutoring in schools and universities and recruitment advice where you can get career guidance on where you want to go next.

However, the World Happiness Report also noted that personal freedom is not without its challenges. Sometimes personal freedom can conflict with other important values, such as social justice, equality and security. For example, the freedom to accumulate wealth and power may lead to increased inequality and social division, while the freedom to express hateful or harmful views may undermine the rights and dignity of others.

You can see this at work when considering the conflict in the Middle East, which has raised its head again as I am writing this book. Universally, no matter where you are, people are supporting one or the other side. Yet, no matter who you support, you are vilified for speaking up. In Finland, there has been much discussion on politicians' freedoms when showing support for causes they believe in. They might support a particular cause as an individual, for example, such as animal rights. However, as a politician, they are cautioned against openly expressing their personal views.

What I want you to understand is that Finland scores 100 out of 100 for freedom of speech generally, as per the *Freedom House report*. However, there are examples of bullying happening against more open journalists and politicians who go off-piste with their opinions and articles.

The World Happiness Report emphasises the need for a balanced approach to personal freedom that considers the broader social and ethical implications of individual choices and actions. In Finland, you have very strong freedom of speech. You may express yourself and I believe most Finns do so ethically. However, like in the example above with online abuse of public figures raising their voices, Finland is not immune to times when freedom of speech turns out badly. Some people choose the other less ethical path. And let's not forget internet trolls are everywhere.

Overall, the World Happiness Report 2023 highlights the importance of personal freedom as a key determinant of happiness and well-being. By promoting greater levels of personal freedom, while also balancing the needs of broader social and ethical considerations, societies can create a fairer and more fulfilling environment for all individuals.

While an *optimistic* mindset is an important factor in helping Finland take the number one spot in happiness rankings, a *resilient* mindset is equally involved. Let's take a look at *sisu*, the Finnish form of resilience.

"Sisu will get you
even through
granite"
Finnish proverb

CHAPTER 2

Sisu, the Finnish resilience

isu is a uniquely Finnish concept that describes the mindset of perseverance, determination and resilience in the face of challenges. It is a combination of grit, tenacity and courage, and it has played a significant role in Finnish history and culture. The term sisu comes from the Finnish word sisukas, meaning someone who has an inner strength, courage and perseverance – to overcome obstacles and achieve their goals.

Sisu is not just about being tough or stubborn but having the mental and emotional fortitude to push through difficulties and keep going, even when the odds are against you.

Sisu is also about having a sense of purpose and meaning. This means *sisu* is a mindset that can be learned and developed. It can also apply to various aspects of life, not just dark times, including work, relationships and personal challenges. And for me, it is the tendency of not giving up when everyone else around you is losing hope.

In this chapter, we will explore the origins and meaning of *sisu* and how it has contributed to Finnish happiness and success. We will also examine the characteristics of the *sisu* mindset, such as perseverance, determination, courage and resilience.

I am not the first to write about *sisu*. There are lots of books describing this word and its meaning to us Finns. You can find a list of great reads in the back of this book, if you'd like more books on this topic.

Let's start with an example from my life. In 2012, I was trying to obtain my private pilot licence here in Australia, but I realised I could not finish it until after I gave birth to my first son. I had continued flying until I was too big to pull the stick back in my small four-seater Cessna. I had to pause my flying practice until after my son was born – much to the relief of my instructors! Three months after I had my son in December 2012, I was back to flying; a few months after that, I passed my last practical exam and could call myself a pilot. My instructor laughed when I told him – on that same flight – that I was pregnant with my second child. He was more relieved than I was that I had passed the exam!

Many others would have given up flying when other life events happened. Yes, I had a baby, but I also had to time my flying lessons in between feeding times! The thing is that I did not even once think about giving up what I'd set out to achieve. I badly wanted to have my pilot licence. And I knew I could and would get it. The whole time, I thought about it with this attitude: I will get the licence no matter how long it takes.

This is a form of resilience too, because *sisu* is also about long-term goals and how having perseverance gets you through anything.

Sisu is deeply ingrained in Finnish culture and has played a significant role in shaping the country's history and identity. We have described it as a 'secret weapon' of the Finnish people, helping us overcome adversity and achieve success in various fields.

One example of *sisu* in action is the Winter War of 1939–1940, when Finland was attacked by the Soviet Union. Despite being vastly outnumbered and outgunned, the Finnish army fought valiantly for 105 days, demonstrating incredible resilience and determination. The Finnish people also showed their *sisu* by persevering through the harsh winter conditions and shortages of food and supplies.

But *sisu* is not just limited to extraordinary feats of bravery and endurance. It is also a mindset that can apply to everyday challenges and obstacles. For example, a person with *sisu* might approach a hard task with a 'never give up' attitude, and view setbacks as opportunities to learn and grow.

I have pulled out my *sisu* attitude many times over the years. When I wanted to move to Australia and it would not happen, I drew on my inner strength and persevered. When I ruptured the ACL in my knee and had to work out how to parent with one leg and crutches when my hubby was working for a while, talk about multitasking but more so talk about *sisu*! I really needed my 'you can do it' attitude.

Another time, I was living in Sydney when I had to dig into my *sisu*. I had had my first son and was feeling like a prisoner in my home. The location was great. The house was everything and more. Still, I was not happy. The busy area – with people, cars, grumpy neighbours and all – added to my feelings of isolation. I needed a change, as I did not see my kids growing up where we were. I did not feel it was the right place for myself or my family. So, we set off looking for a house outside Sydney. I persevered and found my happy place.

That is when we found the little bubble of heaven, my

very own Arctic Paradise where we live now, on the south coast of New South Wales.

So, how do you cultivate a *sisu* mindset? How does resilience apply to everyday life so that you can increase your level of happiness?

Personally, I always feel grounded when I have goals. Goals give you a sense of purpose. Every action we take towards our goals requires us to practice optimism and gratitude, as well as embrace challenges and setbacks. *Sisu* is a crucial mindset for achievement. And setbacks are just opportunities for even more growth.

In terms of its contribution to happiness and well-being, *sisu* can help individuals develop a sense of self-efficacy, which can lead to greater confidence, optimism and satisfaction with life. The persistence and determination associated with *sisu* can help individuals achieve their goals and overcome obstacles, leading to a greater sense of accomplishment and purpose.

Like writing a book! (Here I should insert a smiley emoji because of how many times I have had to restart this project!) When my first draft was destroyed by the computer that died and I had not saved it to the cloud... *sisu*! When I wanted to throw the computer through the window several times when I was stuck and could not move forward with my project... *sisu*! These are times when I looked inside of myself and called up on my inner resilience.

"We all have these moments when we all need to reach beyond what we think we are capable of. At the end of physical, emotional and psychological endurance. And then we have some kind of force that allows us to continue even when we thought we couldn't," says Emilia Lahti, author and researcher of *sisu* as positive psychology. I reflected on her words when I just could not see the end of writing this book, because I knew

I *could* do it; I just had to pull on my big girl pants and get on with it.

When you want to cultivate a *sisu* mindset, it can involve various strategies, such as setting challenging goals, developing a positive mindset, practicing self-compassion and seeking support from others. By embracing *sisu*, individuals can develop the inner strength and resilience needed to navigate life's challenges and pursue their dreams, leading to greater happiness and fulfilment. So you see, *sisu* is an integral part of Finnish happiness. They might not measure it in the World Happiness Report, but it truly is the backbone of a happy life.

Another important aspect of *sisu* is its connection to personal values and a sense of purpose. When individuals clearly understand their values and goals, it can provide a sense of direction and motivation, which can help them overcome obstacles and stay focused on what matters most.

Of course, there is also the aspect of *sisu* that focuses on perseverance and determination. When faced with challenges or setbacks, individuals with a *sisu* mindset are more likely to persist and keep trying. This can be especially valuable in situations where success may require sustained effort over a long period.

I always tell my sons about *sisu* when they are about to give up on a task, a sport or something they are meant to do for school. My youngest wanted to give up on learning to swim. He kept having tantrums and refusing to go to the swimming pool. We had to work hard to get him to first enjoy swimming; secondly, to understand that this skill would give him more in his life than not being able to swim; and thirdly, to know that it might save his life one day! I talked about how we never give up, that he has *sisu* blood in him and he will do this. Finally, after many sessions of trying to convince him, he got back to the pool and enjoyed it. Once he enjoyed it, he started learning again. He is not the fastest swimmer now, but he knows how to swim, which was the goal.

Sisu can also contribute to greater resilience in the face of adversity. When individuals have a strong sense of inner strength and self-efficacy, they are better equipped to cope with stress and difficulty. I have to say that I rarely if ever get stressed about anything in life. I just think life happens. You cannot control everything. You just have to get on with things. Having this attitude towards stress can lead to greater emotional well-being and a more positive outlook on life.

Sisu is not just a Finnish concept. We can find similar ideas in other cultures and traditions, such as the Japanese concept of *ganbaru* or the American idea of *grit*. By embracing the principles of *sisu*, individuals from all backgrounds can develop the inner strength and resilience needed to pursue their goals and lead a happy, fulfilling life.

Besides perseverance, *sisu* is also associated with courage and bravery. This can involve taking risks, facing fears and standing up for what you believe in. You hear kids calling someone *sisukas* in the playground when their friend has done something particularly awesome against the odds. By demonstrating courage in these circumstances, when not expected to succeed, individuals with a *sisu* mindset can build confidence and self-esteem, which in turn contributes to happiness and well-being again.

Finnish kids get resilience ingrained in them from early on. One example I can think of is using *sisu* in times of homesickness when young people are sent to church-arranged youth camps. I went on one in my early teens and recall how exciting it was to go to this summer camp with my sister and be miles away from home. The place was by the lake and there were old train carriages turned into cabins. I remember staying there because of *sisu* and learning not to miss home so much but be excited by these experiences instead.

Sisu is not just a mindset for individuals; it is a cultural value in Finland. By supporting the principle of *sisu* at the societal level, Finland has created a culture that values resilience, determination and personal responsibility. This has contributed to a strong sense of social cohesion and well-being among Finnish people. Finland has built a culture of *sisu* at the community level and following suit can be a powerful way to tap into your own resilience, determination and personal responsibility.

By learning from the Finnish example, individuals from all backgrounds can cultivate a *sisu* mindset and build the resilience and determination needed to achieve their goals and lead a happy, fulfilling life.

HOW TO HAVE MORE *SISU* IN YOUR LIFE

Here are some specific examples of what you can do to promote *sisu* in your own life.

PHYSICAL CHALLENGES

Examples include: running a marathon, completing a multiday hiking expedition, or competing in an endurance race such as a triathlon. These activities require significant physical and mental stamina, so they can help individuals develop a sense of resilience and determination. If running is not your thing, just start challenging yourself. Rather than taking the straightforward route for your next walk, maybe walk longer and further. Even baby steps count in the end.

CREATIVE CHALLENGES

Examples include: writing a novel, completing a challenging art project, or learning to play a musical instrument. These activities require sustained effort and dedication, so they can help individuals develop a sense of perseverance and self-efficacy. With any of these examples, you learn a new skill that can help you further in life.

SOCIAL CHALLENGES

Examples include: volunteering for a cause, organising a community event, or taking part in a group that promotes a

shared interest or goal. Being part of a group, community or organisation gives the sense of belonging. This, in turn, can create contentment in your life and give you a sense of social support. (I talk about things such as volunteering later in this book.)

INTELLECTUAL CHALLENGES
Examples include: learning a new language, pursuing an advanced degree, or mastering a complex skill, such as coding or data analysis. These activities require sustained effort and dedication too. I can only concur here! While writing this book, I started a course with Cambridge University on Business Sustainability. Why, you might ask. Not that I was bored or anything, but I felt a need to stretch myself and my knowledge that little bit further.

Overall, any activity that requires sustained effort and dedication, and involves some challenge or risk, can help promote a strong *sisu* mindset. By embracing these activities and pushing yourself beyond your comfort zone, you can develop the inner strength and resilience needed to pursue your goals and lead a happy, fulfilling life.

You do not need to live in Finland to bring this aspect of happiness into your life. You always have access to *sisu* when you find the determination to get things done.

Let's leave determination and resilience for a while and turn to a lighter subject... The Finnish sense of generosity and how it relates to people being less corruptible.

"Finland was ranked as the second least corrupt country in the world behind Denmark 2023."

CHAPTER 3

Lack of Corruption

The Nordic countries, including Finland, are known for having low levels of corruption compared with other parts of the world. There are several reasons these countries have been able to maintain relatively high levels of integrity in their public and private sectors.

One key factor is the culture of transparency and openness that is prevalent in our Arctic Paradise. Governments, businesses and civil society organisations in these countries place a high value on accountability and information-sharing. There are strong legal frameworks in place to support these values. For example, many Nordic countries have solid freedom of information laws that guarantee citizens the right to access government documents and other types of information.

Another important factor is the high social trust that exists in these countries. Trust is a critical ingredient for a functioning democracy and a healthy economy, as it allows individuals to cooperate and collaborate with one another and to believe that others will act in good faith. Finland has built up this trust over time through a combination of factors, including strong social safety nets, high levels of social equality, and a culture of consensus-building and compromise.

Finland has also implemented strong anti-corruption measures that have helped to keep corruption levels low. These measures include robust legal frameworks for detecting and punishing corrupt behaviour, as well as independent oversight bodies that monitor public and private institutions for signs of corruption. For example, Finland has a specialised anti-corruption agency, the National Bureau of Investigation, which investigates and prosecutes corruption cases.

In Australia, I see allegations of corruption appear in the media comparatively often. While it is not the case that corruption never happens in Finland, we do know it is less frequent.

The last measure to mention is that Finland has a way of promoting ethical behaviour and good governance in all sectors of society. The good governance model, which includes trust and self-reporting, comprises pillars that promote transparency and accountability in the private sector, as well as initiatives to promote ethical behaviour and prevent conflicts of interest among public officials. Self-reporting of any issues is made easy to implement in Finland: every government institution has the option to self-report on their website. In general, being a whistleblower is not frowned upon but applauded.

Trusting the government and the society you live in is a strong reason to be happy in Finland. Perhaps most common amongst all the Nordic countries is our institutions' openness to criticism. The public sector receives criticism, feedback and complaints, and they take the feedback on board.

Change through the lens of feedback is never a bad thing; it only makes us do better. Again, comparing this with Australia, whistleblowing is newer and there are fewer measures in place for how organisations should handle this. If you are a whistleblower, you are sure to be targeted.

Finland has been able to maintain relatively low levels of corruption, while we may not easily replicate these factors in other parts of the world, they offer valuable lessons on how to build more integrity and trust in public and private institutions.

I have never come across a dodgy officer or a decision that I thought was not right when dealing with Finnish institutions. It is unheard of that someone would not do the right thing. Among other things, a marker of happiness is living in a place where you can trust that officials have your best interests in mind.

And if you can't trust officials where you live, what can you do about it? There is always complaining, calling out people who do wrong and voting in people who represent a change in the next elections.

Generosity

Related to trust and integrity, another important aspect of a happiness mindset is gratitude. Gratitude refers to the practice of being thankful for what we have, rather than focusing on what we lack. When you have a solid foundation of people doing the right thing, it is easier to relax and notice more and more of what is right in the world. And from that place, we can be more generous, because we see how very abundant we are.

Happiness research has shown that individuals who regularly practice gratitude are happier, more optimistic and more satisfied with their lives. This is because gratitude helps us shift our focus away from negative thoughts and emotions and appreciate the positive aspects of our lives.

Finns are grateful for: the Arctic Paradise, pure nature that we can call home, wandering about foraging mushrooms and berries, enjoying the taste of your morning coffee by the lake house, sitting outside watching the sunset...

And we want to share our happiness with you as well!

On one of our early trips to Finland, my husband was 'kidnapped' by my friends and taken to a sauna. He did not know what to think about this, downing beers, naked, with mates you just met who behave like they have known you all your life! He later said it was an uncomfortable feeling, but he braved through it. He said we Finns like to share a little too much; I take it he was talking about what he saw in the sauna.

However, generosity can be more than just offering a beer in a sauna. It is about listening, being there for each other. Generosity of giving back. Opening a door, looking after the elderly, saying hello to a neighbour. These are small gestures, but they mean a lot. How do you practice these acts of kindness in your life?

When I was studying to become a nurse, I was an active volunteer with Red Cross Finland. I did first aid courses with them; I facilitated first aid coverage of public events. I also did a ski slope first aid course to help bring patients down on a sledge when there were injuries. These examples of giving back, creating a network of connections and volunteering are the core of what makes people happier than average. I believe that just being present in other people's lives, giving back your time, knowledge or experience makes you and the receiver happier in life.

WAYS TO GIVE BACK GENEROUSLY

Here are some more ways you can give back from a place of generosity.

VOLUNTEER
Give your time to worthy causes that you care about, like a neighbourhood patrol, school parent committee, sport team or working as a volunteer in a hospital or an organisation you are passionate about.

GIVE BACK
Putting it simply, give financial aid to those in need. Pick a charity and contribute to them on a regular basis.

MENTORING OR TUTORING
Share knowledge about what you are good at with young kids who need extra academic support.

ASSISTING ELDERLY OR DISABLED PEOPLE

Enrich their lives with your life skills, helping with household chores or simply spending time listening to them.

Giving back forces you to live in the moment as well. How can you have a more content life living in the moment? This is what we'll cover next.

"Happiness is being with my dogs and surrounded by animals, who know how to appreciate the moment. Sitting in front of the fire with a hot cup of cocoa or glass of red wine, feeling and being at peace, not thinking about my to-do list. Nothing to do with material things – those are just fleeting."

Arctic Grub

CHAPTER 4

Living the Moment

We Finns are great at living in the moment, like sitting on a seat in the sauna where you just enjoy *being* there. There are no digital distractions, no need to go anywhere, do anything, just stay right where you are enjoying the sweat dripping off you and letting the heat to tend to your aching muscles after a day's work. Finns believe you leave your worries behind and things that bother you roll away through sweating. In other words, sweating heals.

Happiness does not need to be complicated. It can be just that – enjoying what you have. When I read about happiness, and how Finland and Finnish people define it, one common theme kept coming up. Happiness is a very wide concept for something that Finns consider as merely *satisfaction for what you have in life*. We do not talk about happiness in the same way the World Happiness Report does. Happiness is a big word – even too big. We are almost afraid to say it out loud!

Instead, we Finns talk about contentedness or simply satisfaction. We say we are satisfied with life. Not happy, just satisfied. We might have been branded the happiest country in the world, but we think we are merely *satisfied* with life and *content* with what we have. That is the inner humble Finn coming out here. Humility is a Finnish quality I love to embrace. Personally, I think we are the humblest people in the world; though you do not get a badge for being humble!

In an article about happiness, I found the following saying: "*Satisfaction in life does not equal happiness.*" This phrase stared out at me from the page. What did they mean? I wondered. Intrigued, I started to research and talk to fellow Finns about how they viewed happiness and what it meant to them. I got answers from one extreme to the other and everything in between.

Many said that the World Happiness Report only measured the satisfaction of services the government does or does not provide. It did not talk about genuine happiness – being in sync with nature, sustainability, opinions and thoughts that can be freely expressed, feeling free. For many people, happiness was not materialistic or monetary support that the government could provide. It was about your own happiness, living in the moment, having a content outlook in life.

When looking at how Finns live in the moment, we can now define happiness as Finns really see it. As I've said, it is not about materialistic goods; instead, happiness is a *state of mind*. How you look at what you have, how you feel about yourself. Finnish happiness is about the small things in life.

For a Finn, happiness is when you sit by the lake after a sauna watching the birds fly over a mirror of calm waters, listening to the surrounding nature with a cold beer in your hand. There is no one else there, just you and the moment, a picture-perfect Arctic Paradise. You centre yourself in the moment and just enjoy being there. That is real happiness, according to many Finns. Yes, I know I mentioned beer. More about alcohol-infused happiness later in this book, because we cannot avoid talking about the fact that Finns love to drink.

For some people, this picture-perfect moment would require taking a pic for Insta and posting on their feed. Or having music pumping in the background with a party ready to start. Or dancing on the beach with friends. Or having a barbecue in the background with busy family and friends. These could 'spoil' your moment. Yet some, or even all of these, equal happiness to someone. It is subjective and up to you how you feel and experience it.

Happiness is many things for many people, but for Finns it is always these small things, being with yourself and enjoying the moment.

How can we measure happiness though? How can we measure the examples I have used here, which are based on your own experience, on how you perceive the moment? Do we measure how many of these moments we have per length of time? How intense they are? How long they last? As you can see, the Finnish definition of happiness is not something we can measure easily. If you go too long without a sauna, you definitely become miserable, I say, so perhaps that is the Finnish way to measure happiness!

Here's one way we won't be measuring it... If I took you to Finland, something people always notice and comment on is the lack of Finnish people smiling. We do not walk around with a permanent smile on our faces, like perhaps people do in some other nations. And no, I am not pointing a finger at our Swedish neighbours. I assure you this does not mean that Finns are not happy. We just do not need to express it to everyone all of the time. Displaying emotions is not something that you get out of Finns easily.

"Smiling without reason? Why would you do that?" my Finnish friend and I would laugh and joke when we talked about the 'stoic' expressions we Finns have on our faces. "It's resting bitch face," my friend suggested. I disagreed. It's not that we look *unhappy*. We just do not show our emotions at all, even when *happy*. Happiness for Finns does not equal smiling.

For my North American friends, I know this might be difficult to accept, but here it is... Finns can be happy and content without smiling! Having a sauna or sitting by the lake with no smile on our faces, it's possible!

My husband attended a Finnish party many years ago in London. Being a Brit, he had thought conservative amounts of happiness might at least be on display. However, he got frustrated and started asking people if they were happy since no one was smiling. People thought he was weird. I thought it was funny. He was trying to provoke emotions out of Finns, making them smile, but even his best efforts did not pay off. The party people avoided him after that and he only got more agitated. In the end, I took the liberty of removing us from the premises. You get the picture, I'm sure.

Afterwards, he said he had never met such a bunch of miserable people in his life. In his defence, he had not yet spent time in Finland. This was early on when we'd just started going out. It took me a while to explain that we do not smile like a fool 'just because'. You need to get to know us to earn our smiles.

Nature

We Finns love nature. We cannot live without it. Being outside relaxes you and recharges you, making you happy and content. You will see Finns walking, hiking, skiing, cycling, skating and just moving around the town no matter the weather.

I recall one sunny day where the sun was shining so bright on the winter snow that it hurts your eyes. I was walking from my friends' place to my student accommodation a few kilometres away. However, I did not have my sunglasses on. Before I got to my place, my eyes were watering, everything was blurry and I could barely see where I was going. I was going snow blind but couldn't close my eyes because I wouldn't be able to see where I was going.

I ended up going into the nearest shop and buying some sunglasses, which I could not really afford on my student budget. Still, I would not have been able to get home without them. I stopped for a coffee with another friend and gave my eyes a rest. By the time I had finished my chat and drink, the weather had changed. It was not sunny, no blue sky. There was a gale blowing and snow drift coming in sideways. I still walked home... no sunnies on my face though!

That day, I recall thinking how the weather could change so fast, but instead of being unhappy about it, I could just walk home as planned and feel content about that. Accepting the fate of being cold, wet and needing a sauna at home, I actually felt invigorated, from being outside, seeing a friend and experiencing the changes I had just seen.

Nature makes us who we are. We need nature like we need oxygen to breathe. It helps us live in the moment.

"I have concluded that basic satisfaction / happiness is based on living closer to the rhythm of nature."
Mari Katariina

When I asked in a Finnish Facebook forum about happiness, I received this comment, which was a lightning bolt moment for me. I think Mari Katariina is right. Finnish happiness, feeling content with life, is linked with nature, the seasons and the rhythm of life.

And how seasons change! That is their nature. From summer to autumn, we see leaves changing colour, we forage for berries and mushrooms, and we start getting ready for the hunting season. We add more layers of clothes, we put away summer shoes, and we take out the sturdier, water-repellent ones from the closet. From autumn to winter, you get the feeling of the first snow falling and it's something everyone talks about; it even gets broadcast in the media as to how many centimetres we'll get around the country from the first of the season's snow.

The rhythm of the seasons is part of the Finnish psyche. Are we happier or more content in the summer when the sun is out and does not go down? Or are we happier and more content in the middle of winter when we have less light but more time at home to potter around, ski, enjoy crisp snow under our shoes and the spring sun on our skin?

Many Finns miss the sun, it's true. And there are definitely those who have sun and summer in their hearts. However, I miss the snow and cooler weather. I feel I was made to live when it is snowing and enjoy myself the most when it's cooler here in Australia.

The rhythm of life is linked to nature. Just look at the birth of babies. There is a clear pattern of when babies are 'made'. In Finland, birth rates peak in September, nine months after New Year, and mid-March, nine months after midsummer. I am a March baby and my sister is a September baby. I say no more than that my parents' wedding anniversary is in June!

THINGS THAT HELP YOU LIVE IN THE MOMENT

How can you get more nature in your life so you can live in the moment more? My best advice is to use nature as a way to:

RECHARGE YOUR BATTERIES

By living closer to the earth, by walking in the park, exploring your neighbourhood and noticing what nature you can see.

REST YOUR MIND

You feel more rested and centred in nature. More endorphins flow in your body and you are happier for it.

DO A DIGITAL DETOX

No gimmicks, no digital devices required. Just you taking a walk, exploring and being in the moment.

GET OUTDOORS

No secret sauce, but trust me! If you have not been used to getting outside and breathing the morning sunshine, get out there before you regret it. It is never too late to start new habits of how to start your day.

"I always joke that I actually grew up in the woods and played with sticks and picked blueberries straight from the bush – this kind of upbringing in the UK is utopia and I think it affects the mind differently to growing up in a concrete jungle."

Julia V

CHAPTER 5

Freedom for Children

I n my own school years, I loved history, geography and many other subjects. I had outstanding teachers – some that still make me think, *'Wow, I got to learn skills that serve me even today'*. It gave me a love for history, trying to understand geography and biology, and how our past affects the present day and the future we are building.

I had a particular teacher I liked. He was my history teacher in my early teens. He made all of us love history. The entire class really dug into history because of him. This teacher got us. He could demonstrate how history related to today's world. For example, he showed us how today's French society is still based on those early days of the French Revolution when people barricaded the streets of Paris in the 1790s shouting, "Liberté, égalité, fraternité!" He taught us how these words are still echoed on coins, buildings and societal reforms in the present day.

I did my school years in a small town. At seven years old, I took the bus to school and back independently. The half hour bus drive was actually my favourite way to see friends and get together before we headed into school. We'd talk about what we had been doing and what we were going to do on our breaks (a compulsory 15 minutes for every hour of learning).

I always remember the emphasis on ski days when we would take our skis and go for a ski outside the town. It was nice to have everyone on skis and see who could get to the end of the trial first.

The kids of Finland have it good. So good that they do not even know it! Let's face it, free school meals, free transport to and from school, free books and teaching, all at no cost to families thanks to the Finnish government – that's something I think Finns take for granted. These kids are happy without knowing it. They are content with the school programme, how school has been laid out in front of them. They just need to turn up. Pretty easy, right?

Finnish education is so good that it is an export. Kide Science and Code School Finland are few examples of where Finland's educational knowledge is exported overseas. There is great demand for this, particularly in Asia and North America.

My sister being an English teacher in Finland taps into my knowledge and more so my kids' knowledge by getting my sons to talk to her class in Finland via the web. My kids love the interaction and ask questions of the students, in turn answering the questions my sister's class have for them.

Sport is often a universally common interest. The kids in Finland do skiing, ice hockey and soccer, whereas my kids in Australia do surfing, mountain biking and rugby. Our life is so exotic for them and their life is exciting to us!

From these discussions, one thing is clear though: how much these kids are happy to walk, bike or get the bus to school and back on their own with no parental supervision.

Yes, shock horror! Kids walk, bike and take public transport to and from school on their own in Finland, because it is safe to do so.

In Finland, the freedom kids have is one of those things many foreigners look at with fear in their eyes. "Does your kid really go to school on their own?" or "Do you really leave your prams outside in the cold in the middle of winter while the baby sleeps?" The answer is yes to both questions!

When thinking about contentment in Finnish society and how Finns tend to be happy, we need to revisit that broader concept of trust. The question becomes how we can trust people around us, whether that is strangers on the bus, people at work, your neighbours, friends or family.

As we have seen and as the World Happiness Report says, trust is a major factor of happiness:

> *"The Nordic countries have the highest well-being, though they are not richer than many other countries. But they do have higher levels of* trust *and of mutual respect and support."*

Finns trust each other more than perhaps people in other countries do. We have learned to trust each other from early on when we trust our neighbours. We rely on each other, as demonstrated in this example. Finns build houses only in spring and summer, when the permafrost has melted enough to lay foundations in the ground. When building a house, the entire village will turn up to help lay the concrete or lift the frame.

Similarly, Finland's neighbouring countries, Sweden and Norway, have needed us throughout the centuries, just as we have needed them. As such, we know we always have each other's back in our Arctic Paradise.

We teach our kids this same trust: that you can trust adults around you, that the village you need is just *there*, in the neighbouring houses, as well as in society more generally.

Another contributor to happiness that kids have and do not even realise is the freedom to move around, go places and experience life, exploring the parks, wildlife, neighbourhood and your mate's back garden.

Pasi Sahlberg, Finnish educator and scholar, said in an interview with Green Mountain Community School in Australia:

> *"Children come to school with different interests, different capabilities, potentials and talent. What a school needs to do is to try to help every single child to realise what it is for them, what they love, what they're good at, etc. Sometimes you need to try a number of times, to dig deep into the souls of these young children so they can realise 'this is what I really want to do', 'this is what I am curious about' so that children don't go through school without realising what they are good at."*

For some kids in different countries, this is not the case. They may not explore their surroundings in their community as it is not a secure and safe thing to do. These kids might live in war zones, neighbourhoods with high crime or other unsafe environments.

Finnish children do not have that problem. Children as young as six or seven travel alone by bus, taxi, train and metro. It is not unheard of that school-age children might take a bus journey across the country to spend time at their grandparents' house at holidays. Parents just put them on the train or bus and off they go with little supervision from the driver.

The resilience that Finnish kids have is a quality that serves them well in life. They learn to trust themselves and their ability to succeed by gaining independence early in life. It is quite okay for parents to leave kids home alone after school for a few hours. There is no need for after-school care or clubs. Kids can return home, make food and do school work until parents come home. Again, it is about the trust factor.

My kids, on the other hand, have grown up in Australia. At the time of writing this, my youngest is turning nine. No way could I leave both boys home for more than an hour! I am envisioning coming home to a pile of ashes. Perhaps the trust between parents and children has not transferred all the way overseas!

Finns teach kids to be resilient too, which in turn gives them a sense of freedom and happiness. Trusting yourself and people around you to make good decisions and do the right thing is important, but it is a scary and unheard-of thing to do in many countries.

Free schooling

What about the schools though? Much has been written about the Finnish school system and how good it is, that Finland is a shining example of how well school can prepare children for the future. I have to say I agree, but I do admit I am a product of the Finnish school system!

I still recall fondly the time I spent in school. I liked school, and it was a safe and nurturing environment to be in. I recall one teacher who told us we wouldn't know how good the Finnish school system is until we weren't in it anymore. She was right!

How does free schooling relate to happiness then? Well, one less thing that parents have to worry about, for one. Schools are all designed to be equal in terms of quality of teaching, no matter where you are in Finland, where you were born, what kind of background you come from. You may have free school wherever and whoever you are. Prime Minister Sanna Marin came from a very usual upbringing in Finland and was raised in a very average suburb of Tampere. She did well at school and made it to university to study law, one of the hardest courses to get a place.

> *"I feel like the big points after diving in more depth myself regarding Finland being the Happiest country in the world rankings, come down to things like the small income inequality along with a really good and supportive public health system and equitable educational institutions that provide kids with equal opportunities for education and to endeavour their full potentials."*
> Kristiina Roosimaa

You do not have to pay any fees in high school, polytechnic or university either, which is perhaps the reason why the lifelong learning concept prevails in Finnish society. Finns like to learn and invest in themselves. We are avid readers. And as any reader knows, reading makes you happy!

Finns believe happiness is gained from citizens that are well-educated and who can contribute something towards society. Receiving education, free schooling and school meals can enhance the well-being of individuals in the education sphere.

As a parent who does not have access to Finnish school, I can say education in Australia does still have its perks, but I would love the schools here to have more of the freedom that Finland has. For parents, the Finnish school system really works, because your kids are not only taken care of while you work, but kids become independent and may gain resiliency skills.

"We have an excellent education system. We have a good healthcare and social welfare system that allows anybody to become anything. This is probably the reason Finland gets ranked the happiest country in the world."
Sanna Marin, Prime Minister of Finland

I went through the Finnish school system in the 1980s and '90s, and I recall few things that I think of fondly even today.

First were the free school meals. I did not think that this was anything special until I started preparing lunchboxes as a mum here in Australia. I could not believe that there was no free food for kids in school. How could this be? We had really got used to good things in Finland. When packing the lunches for my kids, I realised that they would not be getting a warm meal (unless a thermos lukewarm dinner from last night counts?) until the evening.

My Finnish friends had warned me what to expect in Australian schools, but it was still a shock. Someone mentioned that kids don't need a warm meal in the daytime here as the weather is hot and nobody would want one, but that meal at lunchtime is fuelling the brain to learn in the afternoon. I questioned whether a vegemite sandwich was really enough. I didn't think so. I tried not to feel bad and instead give my kids the best possible lunchbox I could – with a variety of foods, fruit and vegetables, carbohydrates and protein. It was hard to adjust and it is still sinking in! There are parents who send their kids to school with only prepacked food and then wonder why their kids come home wanting chocolate biscuits like their friends rather than eating carrot sticks. I wish I could, but I cannot change the system on my own.

Second was that we did not have compulsory school uniforms. It was explained to me that everyone in Australia was equal and having uniforms means parents do not have to think about how to dress their kids. However, does having a uniform not have the opposite effect as well – that of failing to encourage individuality? Kids are all expected to behave the same, be the same. Similarly, there are little or no individual learning plans, which bothered me more than I wanted to say.

In the end, I allowed my kids to wear uniforms but let them get away with more colourful socks than the school policy suggests, as a sign of defiance.

In Finland, school children could wear the clothes they wanted and express themselves through their clothes. If you were into something – football, ice hockey or a particular band – you could wear their T-shirt or jersey at school. You were not bound by the beliefs of the school. Individuality was celebrated, including through how you wore your clothes.

Perhaps this would be better in schools around the world that have uniforms. Some parents say uniforms are cheaper, as you do not need to think about what your children wear, but what about the kids who come from low-income families that struggle to make ends meet and put food on the table? Getting school equipment and uniforms is an extra expense to them, not less of one.

At university in Oulu, Finland, in the late 1990s, I recall being in lectures and thinking to myself how cool it was that we could choose what we study. I did not finish my degree in

Finland as my journey took me to London to work and then to study something different. However, even the short moment I was in university in Finland, I could see the impressive system, producing quality academics who pushed the country further.

And what about the preschool years before you get to school? In Finland, you have tax-funded early childhood education that includes lots of outdoor time and play. I would say all the education in Finland in the early years is based on play. When a child turns six, they have to attend a compulsory preschool for a year, equivalent to kindergarten in other countries. Children are taught the alphabet but not how to read. Even in this compulsory preschool year, there is much emphasis on play and outdoor activities, and kids have their own individualised learning plan with input from parents and the help of educators.

Preschool is heavily subsidised so it is affordable to families. The Finnish schooling system is really there to help families and parents guide their children towards the best choices in life. The early education and preschool system make it easy for parents to send their kids to school too.

Overall, the Finnish education system supports parents and children – another reason to be happy, you see? Education in Finland provides equal opportunities for all and promotes student-centred and inclusive learning. The system is funded through taxation and considered an integral part of the Finnish welfare state.

I have never really thought about the university system until I did my degree in the UK. I paid for my studies, which I felt was a lot of money at the time. It has paid itself back many times over the course of my life with the work I have done. In a few job interviews, comments were made about me being a 'product of the Finnish education system'. It has definitely been a bonus and got me places.

EMBRACE LIFELONG LEARNING

Do you want to take a leaf out of the Finns' book and stay aware and agile as you age? Here are some ways you can embrace lifelong learning, even if you are a long time past school!

TAKE A FREE COURSE on a subject you are interested in through the Open University, a community college or polytechnic.

DO A SKILL SWAP with a neighbour, colleague or friend.

READ A BOOK about a subject you're interested in.

HIRE A COACH or **JOIN A TEAM** where you can improve a skill you already have.

LEARN AND PRACTICE a new DIY project skill.

I have contemplated studying more and will perhaps do my master's through a Finnish university. So far, work and writing have kept me too busy to fit in the studies, but perhaps one day. Just as Finns have a belief in lifelong learning, remember you are never too old to learn! Throughout your life and as you age, you can keep yourself busy and your brain engaged, learning, coaching and practicing. You will change and improve whatever it is that you set your mind to doing.

Next, we look at social policies and how these contribute to Finnish happiness.

"A child is like a book, where each day is a new chapter full of surprises and joy"

Anonymous

CHAPTER 6

Happiness starts at birth

Before your eyes glass over, hear me out. Finland – and all the Nordic countries, in fact – would not have achieved their status on the happiest country list without very progressive social policies.

Take Finland's baby box policy, for example. You might have heard of this. No, we are not talking about baby boxes like in the US, where you can put your unwanted baby up for adoption. This is a box full of goodies for the mother of every new baby that everyone in Finland is entitled to when they are expecting a child.

Back in the 1920s, Finland had one of the highest infant mortality rates in Europe, if not the world. *Mannerheim League for Child Welfare* was headed by a nurse, who started *kiertokorit*. These were baskets of clothes donated for new mothers.

"These clothes were included with linens and hygiene items into 'rotating baskets' (kiertokorit in Finnish) and

were loaned to local mothers who needed them. After a baby grew out of the clothes, the baskets were returned to the volunteers, who repaired and laundered the contents, then passed them on to the next family."
Wikipedia

A seed of happiness was sown back then, helping those in need in Finnish society. The natal care baskets took over the country and were used by two-thirds of new mothers during wartime. After the war, another programme was cemented with legislation, making maternal and childcare clinics available free of charge to all families. By 1949, all expectant mothers received the baby box when they visited the doctor before the fourth month of the pregnancy.

Even today, there is prerequisite to visit the antenatal clinic, then the expectant mother can receive their baby box in the post. It is no longer a baby basket, but a baby box. This cardboard box is made of recyclable material and has a mattress that can be used for the baby to sleep on. The baby box is an example of progressive social policy and how, over time, an idea has evolved to being what it is today.

And it does not end there. If you do not want to have the baby box – let's say you have had a few baby boxes already with your previous children – you can ask to have the baby box as cash instead. Though the money you get is not enough to get all the products that the box contains, many families that already have a child choose the money option as they can pass on hand-me-down clothes to the younger ones instead.

The box is full of practical things like clothing, feeding bibs, nappies, cloth nappies, a mattress, duvet, sleepsuit, book, socks, romper suit, mittens and booties. There has been some conversation about what is in the box over the years. Kela (short for *Kansaneläkelaitos*), the Finnish social insurance authorities that provide the box, asks for feedback from users on how they find it and what can be done better every year. There used to be a bottle for feeding, though this has been taken out to encourage breastfeeding. Hygiene products for mothers are included. There are even condoms, something that would cause outcry in more conservative countries. In Finland, it is accepted as just what it is: to help the new parents on their way.

Again, this shows how our Arctic Paradise society takes care of basic needs and beyond. One more thing to be happy about, I say.

In recent interviews, there has been talk that babies should not sleep in the box anymore. It used to be deemed safer to sleep the baby in the box, rather than in a bed, but nowadays most parents sleep their baby in a cot. The idea of a cot, bassinet or Moses basket being used to sleep the baby is more modern; a baby box might be too old-fashioned for some.

Has the time come to upgrade the baby box offer from the Finnish government to something else more practical for today's needs? Would postnatal classes be more in sync with the times? Or pilates and yoga to help women get back their fitness? Or free babysitting services so that parents can go out? I don't know, but perhaps there is a need to think how this concept can continue to be relevant in today's world and help parents more.

My thoughts on revising the baby box are driven by what I have seen here in Australia and what mothers are asking for most in those early days and weeks when baby arrives home. There is lots of pressure on mothers to get back to work and still be present with their child.

Before I explore that further, let me tell you a story.

I slept in a baby box...

I remember my mother telling me that – since my sister and brother were sharing a cot – they did not have money or room for another one in the place where we were living. So, a baby box it was for me! Apparently, I slept in the box until it became too small for me and started falling apart. I was literally bashing my way out of the box.

I think any mother would be happy to receive such a thoughtful and practical gift as a baby box when starting their journey as a parent. I know I kicked myself when I said no to my mum sending one for my son when he was born. As a Finn, my mother could have bought one from KELA and sent it over to Australia for me.

At the time, there was no commercial businesses producing their own version of the box as there is today. When I had

my second son in 2014, I started to think about starting my own business, but I did not know what exactly. While coming home from the dentist on a bus, I thought: *'What are some good things from Finland that we can bring to the world?'* And yes! The baby box was one of them.

There and then, I googled to make sure no one else was doing the same thing. Nope, there was nothing. So, I started a baby box company here in Australia in 2016 with my Finnish friend Laura.

I ran the company for a few years bringing the baby box concept to Australia. Even though we had good success here, it became very clear that the only place we were going to get commercial success was in a programme run with an indigenous group. The box was not a mainstream product. It was niche. And the education that came with the box was more directed towards families in lower socioeconomic circumstances. That is what the box was initially meant to be, after all: a way to educate and help low-income families and make sure they attended prenatal appointments.

I became aware that state governments were not going to adopt the policy and implement the baby box here in Australia. First of all, questions were asked about the safety of the boxes. It had been serving Finnish parents for decades, but Australian officials were questioning the safety of babies sleeping in boxes – something I took for granted.

When an official asked me, "How does the baby breathe in the box?", it dawned on me that they were crazily – and incorrectly! – thinking that the box lid was on when the baby was inside sleeping! This is when I realised people would

LEFT *Finnish Baby Box by KELA that all mothers in Finland get.*

require a lot of information to educate them about the concept and convert them into fans.

After running the company for few years and realising that we would not be turning the heads of the authorities, I closed the company. It was a bittersweet moment, as I had poured my heart and soul into it, as had my friend Laura. Afterwards, all I could do was lie on the sofa reading books for two weeks. We had just moved to this beautiful seaside town and I had not even been to the beach. I had been working on the business and the world had been going on around me. I had not even stepped onto the sand in the place where we now lived!

I commiserated with myself, then picked myself up off the sofa. I had to let go of that business if I was to create something new. But sometimes, I still wonder *what if...*

What if we had done things differently? What if we had changed some of the products in the box? What if we had had a more niche approach?

I don't know the answer to that and maybe we would have come to the same conclusion anyway. We had to let it go.

Even though the baby box concept did not take off here in Australia, there are many positive examples from around the world of using something similar to the baby box to increase antenatal and prenatal attendance for mothers.

South Africa runs the baby box project as a bag full of goodies for new expecting mothers in several hospital antenatal clinics. These bags are distributed from the hospital clinic, making the mother attend prenatal appointments, hence reducing the likelihood of something going wrong during the pregnancy.

In 2017, Scotland started a baby box programme where boxes full of goodies for the mum and baby were offered to all new mothers. Again, the caveat was attendance at antenatal appointments. The baby box scheme was controversial and seen as a political move by Nicola Sturgeon, the Scottish First Minister at the time. However, it is still going strong and Scotland has made a pledge: "*every baby born in Scotland will be given their own Baby Box.*" The boxes are very much like the Finnish box, with mattress, clothing, etc. Personally, I think Scottish mums get a great gift from their government.

So, the baby box concept that started 100 years ago in Finland shows how equal treatment of children starts from birth. As I said earlier, despite this concept not being taken up here in Australia, I feel something similar could increase the prenatal appointment attendance in lower socioeconomic areas and bring health information to expectant mothers.

These examples reinforce how Finns go about living a content and happy life, where society takes care of your needs and you are better off because of it.

MAKE A BABY BOX

How can babies have happiness from birth if they don't have the Finnish baby box?! If you are a parent, here are some simple things you can try:

ORGANIC CLOTHING

Choose organic cotton or sustainable fabric clothing for your baby, which is gentle on their skin and better for the environment. Look for clothing made from natural fibres and dyed with eco-friendly, nontoxic colours.

TOYS AND ACCESSORIES

Opt for toys made from natural materials, such as wooden toys, organic cotton stuffed animals, or BPA-free, nontoxic plastic alternatives. Explore eco-friendly baby accessories like organic teething rings and silicone-free pacifiers.

SLEEPING YOUR BABY OUTSIDE

It is not a bad thing, according to research from the Nordics, where we tend to sleep our babies in the cold. I used to do the same here in Australia as well by creating a safe and comfortable sleeping environment, allowing the kids exposure to fresh air. Ensure the sleeping area is sheltered from direct elements and temperature extremes.

NATURE EXPLORATION

I was never worried about my children having dirty hands or mud on their faces and clothes. It's natural immunisation against germs, as my mum used to say to us, and I have followed her advice with my kids.

Finland takes care of its babies from before they are born to the day they go to school and beyond. But what about the next stage of life... work-life balance? Is life as easygoing in the Finnish workforce as it is for Finland's children? Are we able to keep things balanced with our other requirements in life? Do we live to work or work to live?

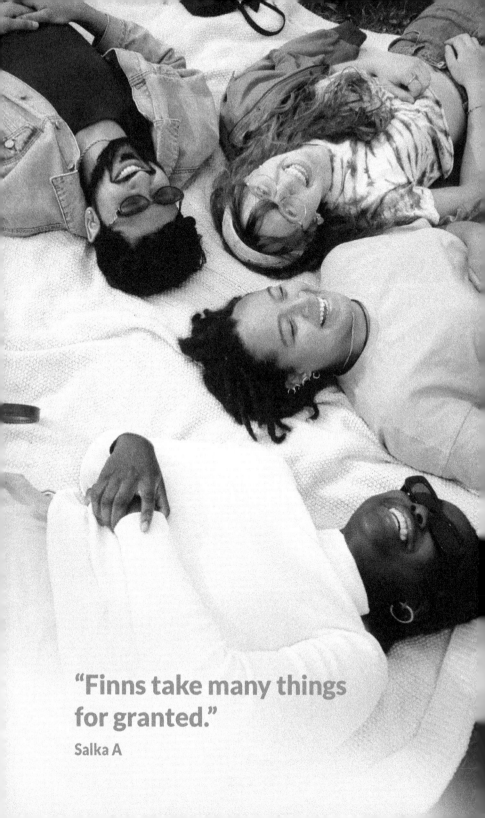

**"Finns take many things
for granted."**
Salka A

CHAPTER 7

Quality of Life

How do you achieve an exceptional quality of life? What do you actually need to be happy? I look at quality of life as something that you achieve little by little. You will not always be 100% happy with what you have. You will always want something more. It's like Christmas dinner, when you go back for seconds, thirds, until you are stuffed and can no longer eat. And then you do not even enjoy the feeling because you are too full.

In life, happiness is a fleeting moment when you are just about full, when you are content. If you stuff yourself silly with Christmas turkey, you do not feel that fleeting moment of happiness – it's all gone turkey with you!

Quality of life belongs in the moments, like we saw earlier. Getting together at Christmas, when it is white with snow outside and ice lanterns guide your family to the house, watching your granny light the candles on the Christmas table. These moments are happiness.

In the Nordics, people embrace the simple things in life and make them important. Take the Swedes, for example, who have *fika*. The concept of *fika* is a coffee and cake, a moment to reflect, enjoy and relax. In Finland too, I remember how nice it was to just be and enjoy these little things. *Pullakahvit* is our Finnish version of coffee and cake, gathering around the table to talk with your loved ones. You need little more than that to be content and enjoy life, right?

Happiness in the small things

When we talk about happiness as being in the moment, are we talking about a love of life that makes us happy people? There are cultures where people are *just happy* the way they are. They don't have money or physical objects to make them happy. People can be happy with less stuff. The amount someone has does not equal happiness.

By accessing untouched places, for example, western countries might think we are going there to educate indigenous people. However, many of those people were content before we arrived. By inserting our values into their reality, we are actually destroying their way of life, not improving it. Oftentimes, not only are people quite content but they are *better off* without our western perspective of what 'quality of life' has to look like.

What makes Finnish people happy? While researching for this book, I have reflected a lot on *what* we need to be happy. Many Finns think Finland is a great place to live. Often, they see their childhood as a reflection of their happiness. Even though I do not live in Finland anymore, I certainly think that way too. Is it idealistic to think that a good childhood leads to lasting happiness, or does the quality of life really come from our upbringing?

Rhythm of nature

We might live in houses, have central heating and enjoying cooked meals in the comfort of our homes, but we are connected to the rhythm of nature more than we think. Perhaps the change of season is one of those things that keeps Finns on their toes. You go from winter to spring, to summer, to autumn, back to winter. You need to change your clothing, your habits and what you eat, how you cook with the season and the hobbies you have. In westernised societies still connected to their roots, we see the connection of children with nature: this is the child who makes snow angels, jumps naked into ice cold water and enjoys every bit of it, laughing all the while.

I saw my boys on a cold winter's day here in Australia making sand angels at the beach and it made me smile, reminding me they really are still wild Finnish boys just living the life here in Australia instead of Finland. They would have done the same with snow angels in Finland, no doubt.

Taking yourself out and enjoying nature is the antidote to feeling glum. There is no doubt in my mind that this is one reason we feel content and happy as Finns. Nature and being connected to it wherever we live makes us happy.

"I have come to the conclusion that basic satisfaction/ happiness is based on living closer to the rhythm of nature, so we are meant to live. We live closer to nature and the basics are sufficiently well taken care of."

Mari Katariina

In Finland, we live close to nature like Mari Katariina says. The country of thousands of lakes has water, forests, parks all around you. Finland has a beautiful natural environment, with plenty of forests, lakes and other natural features. This environment provides opportunities for outdoor recreation and relaxation, which can help to reduce stress and improve mental health.

We embrace flaws and imperfections as part of the natural cycle of life. Appreciation of life – perfect or not – is the core of having quality of life and being happy as an individual.

What about work-life balance? Does Finland have the best working life situation as well? I explore that in the next chapter.

CHAPTER 8

Working Life

D o you work to live or live to work? Let's talk about quality of life in Finland and how working life fits into all this.

I myself have worked very little in Finland. I was doing my nursing studies in the late 1990s when I graduated and dipped my toe into working life in Finland. There was a high unemployment rate amongst nurses at the time and much fighting over shifts. Many nurses had to take casual appointments in the absence of permanent roles and lots of us, like myself, went to work overseas. There was also recruitment in other Nordic countries, as highly skilled Finnish nurses were in demand elsewhere. Many of my colleagues went to live and work in Sweden or Norway and I always thought how easy it was to change countries for work. More distant countries like the United Arab Emirates and Saudi Arabia recruited Finns as well. Us lucky ducks had a such great employment prospects in other countries, just not in Finland.

As I had just finished my studies, I had no work experience.

Any practical training I did hadn't resulted in employment either. Every employer wanted you to have some experience before they would give you shifts. I had to call around and try to cover shifts, which was draining and frustrating. Since I could not find any steady work in Finland, instead of waiting for the employment situation to improve, I left to work in London in the UK.

Before I left though, I signed up to do a degree in geology at the University of Oulu. I wanted to believe that I might become a geologist. We could call it Plan D, if all the other plans failed. I started the course, because like all other Finnish education, this university spot was free. There were no fees to sign up for a degree. All I had to do was sit an exam to get into the university. Once there, I could have studied anything. So, I entertained the idea of this other direction. There was no rush to decide though, and I felt pulled towards a life overseas. I wanted to work, earn my living and be independent. Soon after starting the course, I found myself on a train to Helsinki for an interview with a recruiter from London. I lasted six months at university before moving to the UK.

Despite my personal experience of the Finnish workforce, work-life balance is generally highly valued in Finland and an essential component of a healthy and productive lifestyle. Even though I did not get to enjoy the benefits of Finnish work-life balance, I hear about it from my friends who share their 'hard life' working in Finland. They are very lucky indeed!

Let's begin with working hours. A typical workweek in Finland is 40 hours, with most workers entitled to 30 days of paid holidays each year. Many companies offer flexible work arrangements, such as part-time work or telecommuting, to help employees balance their work and personal lives. Of course, there are expectations that you work hard, but companies get the fact that you may have children, a life outside of your work. Happy employees are the basis of a cheerful company. That pesky word 'happiness' again! The Finns really know how to extend happiness all the way from home to the workplace. Work-life balance is not just about nine to five but nine to thrive.

One thing I really missed by not continuing a career in Finland was the parental leave. In 2012, when I had my son in Australia, I was kicking myself, even though I happily stayed here. We know Finland for its generous parental leave policies, which provide up to 18 weeks of maternity leave and up to 54 weeks of parental leave to be shared between the parents of the baby. This allows new parents to spend time with their newborns and adjust to their new family dynamic. Again, you see what Finland is doing here? Making sure that you are content in our Arctic Paradise so there is no reason to be unhappy or feel like you have to return to work too early.

Sometimes, I have to admit, I look at my Facebook feed with envy towards my friends in Finland. They spend time in resorts at conferences paid for by their employers. Those sunny pictures of skiing with workmates, winter sun on their faces, well, let's just say that we do not get trips like that here in Australia! I do not think some of my Finnish friends realise how good they have it in this regard! How different it can be when you are working with less flexible or unwelcoming employers. How hard it feels in a country where the culture of 'work first and everything else later' will eat you alive, if you cannot keep your head above water.

There used to be a famous summer party for Nokia employees in Finland. It was an employer-paid day out drinking, eating, having fun. It was a full-on day. I recall friends telling me about it. Of course, it was an expensive exercise as there were lots of employees and Nokia would cater for thousands of them. However, the company saw this as an investment in the employees' happiness. By doing this – a party every summer – they were honing the respect and loyalty of their people. Workers would hardly need to look for another employer. I have rarely heard of anyone leaving Nokia during its heyday. They were liked and respected, not only for the perks but for the career prospects as well.

As we spend so much time at work, being happy where you work, being respected and having great colleagues is something we can all embrace. I would ask you to look at your own workplace. What minor changes can be implemented to enhance people's feelings of belonging and contentment? For example, a minor change I can recall that my manager introduced was starting the day with a walk to get coffee with the team. You came along just for the chat. It was not about work so much as you as a person.

HINTS FOR A HAPPIER WORKPLACE CULTURE

As we spend so much time at work, being happy where we work, being respected and having great colleagues is something we can all embrace. I would ask you to look at your own workplace and think about the following:

RECOGNISING ACHIEVEMENTS

Celebrate successes and acknowledge contributions publicly. This could be through shoutouts in meetings, an acknowledgement board, or a monthly newsletter highlighting team achievements.

PROMOTING WORK-LIFE BALANCE

Encourage breaks, time off and flexible working arrangements when feasible. Highlight the importance of mental health and personal well-being. What is your workplace already doing well and what could you do more of?

FOSTERING OPEN COMMUNICATION

Encourage feedback and suggestions from all team members. Implement regular check-ins or anonymous suggestion boxes to gather input on improving the work environment.

AREAS NEEDING IMPROVEMENT

It might be necessary to focus on better communication channels, more diversity and inclusion initiatives, or refining leadership practices to foster a more supportive and empowering work environment.

Try to have some less formal meetings, like an informal chat over coffee or having an activity day with your team. If there are any challenges there, the Finns will take it on! Work-life balance is tied to your overall well-being, which I will talk about next.

"If you eat healthy, happy food you are happier in life."

Anonymous

CHAPTER 9

After having children, I was not taking care of myself very well. Like many parents, I had fallen into the trap of kids first, self last. We had playdates; I had too many croissants and hot chocolates, and well... you get the picture. Although I was walking a lot with my son in the pram, getting from A to B that way, I was not out of breath doing that. However, I definitely wanted to get back to myself. The new mum me, I liked; but the body, I loathed.

I did some running in the evenings when my husband was back from work and I had some time to myself. But I could never really run long distances. I was always that little heavier. I would run half the distance and then walk and then run again. By doing this for a while, I know you start running longer distances, but I never enjoyed running either. I actually hated it. I always felt that my body was not made for running.

So, after having my second son, I realised I really had to get back into shape. I was just ballooning, eating and taking less care of myself than I wanted to admit. Kids came before everything. Then after the house, husband and everything else in between, I was last on the list. Seeing a friend who had three kids effortlessly stepping back to their pre-baby weight, I thought how beautiful those women are – outside and in. I wished that was me, but it wasn't.

A few years ago, I started looking at myself more critically. Yes, I am getting close to the big 5-0 and some things I used to do without any effort had started feeling a little harder. I decided I needed to completely change my lifestyle. Not that I had a dangerous lifestyle, but I had let things slip. And they had slipped for way too long.

I stopped eating so much meat, became flexitarian, getting more fibre and fish into my diet. I also started eating more mindfully. I used to eat breakfast really early when my kids woke up, so by 9 am I was hangry. I stopped having my 'second breakfast' and just had a later one each morning. It

was amazing how this made me feel better. Just pushing my breakfast time from 6 am to closer to 9 am was a monumental shift. I also finished eating a few hours before bedtime. The old saying is that you should not go to sleep with an empty stomach. I lived that dream until I couldn't anymore. I ditched the snacking as well.

I also took up running again. First just down the road, then longer and longer until I could run all the way to the beach with no issues. Now I am looking to incorporate some weight and resistance training into my life.

The point of this story is that you *can* change your habits, if you feel the need to change. Secondly, if you make only one change at a time and stick with it for a few months before making another change, gradual change over time will be more sustainable than lots of changes in a short period.

Well, I dug into *sisu* to get myself started; however, Finns have another great belief that helped me a lot. Finnish people believe that outdoor activities are better for your health and your soul, that health and happiness are intertwined and

physical activity will increase your overall happiness. I feel happier in my body, I am more confident and I can run around with my kids better now than I could a few years ago.

Another thing that we Finns advocate is sauna and a cold dip into the sea or lake. You've seen the ice baths that athletes have after their exercise or game. Cold immersion is good for recovery and we Finns have known that for centuries ever since we started rolling in snow! While a sauna relaxes you and makes your mind wander, melting away the aches, a plunge into icy water or rolling in snow invigorates you and makes you feel alive again. Take whichever makes you feel good. Even better if you do it as a group, because you get the benefits of connecting with other people, which kicks up the endorphins – a sure way to feeling content and happy.

What's food got to do with it?

I was brought up in Finland thinking that good nutritious food can make you happy for several reasons.

- Eating a healthy diet can have a positive impact on your physical health, which can contribute to feelings of happiness and well-being.

- A balanced diet that is rich in fruits, vegetables, whole grains, lean proteins and healthy fats can provide your body with the nutrients it needs to function optimally.

- This can help boost your immune system, reduce your risk of chronic diseases – such as diabetes, heart disease and cancer – and improve your overall energy levels and physical performance.

When you feel physically well, you are more likely to feel happy and content in your daily life.

Besides physical health benefits, good nutritious food can also have a positive impact on mental health. Studies have shown that a diet rich in fruits, vegetables, whole grains and omega-3 fatty acids can help to reduce symptoms of depression and anxiety. Fish and seafood are rich in nutrients such as B vitamins, vitamin D and magnesium, which are important for brain function and mood regulation. These are plentiful in the Finnish diet. On the other hand, you notice the short-term gratification of a sugary treat. After a period of high activity, the sugar effects stop and you want more. For longer-term benefits, ditch the sweet treats and have fruit instead. You will feel better in the long run.

As many Finns do, I always feel happy when preparing and cooking food. The smell of a freshly cooked meal, with freshly baked bread, contributes to feelings of happiness and well-being. In Finland, most people cook homemade meals, and preparing and cooking food together as a family is a treat. In my family, we have pizza nights and it is lovely to have my boys and husband experiment with different ingredients and flavours. Did you know that peas go well on top of pizza? Particularly on a no-cheese pizza with garlic! We love cooking up a storm in the kitchen. It was the same with my mum, who always encouraged cooking and healthy homemade foods, always with a side salad.

The majority of Finns prefer home-cooked food as an enjoyable sensory experience. Fresh, whole foods often have more complex flavours and textures than highly processed foods and can provide a greater sense of satisfaction and pleasure when consumed. The act of savouring and enjoying the flavours and textures, like fresh summer berries, can help to promote a sense of mindfulness and present-moment awareness.

Food Hall in Tampere, Finland where you can get fresh local produce.

Eating strawberries always takes me back to Finland and reminds me of summertime, as that is how summer tastes. We all have those sensory experiences that we associate with happiness. Perhaps yours is a particular food? Or wine? Or dessert? Whatever it is, that sensory experience with food can be experienced again. Your taste buds can contribute to your happiness.

Overall, good nutritious food can make you happy by providing your body with the nutrients it needs to function optimally, reducing your risk of chronic disease, and improving your physical and mental health.

How does the Finnish diet do this? Let's check out what it looks like.

Finnish diet

The Finnish diet is based on a variety of locally sourced and seasonal foods. The country's traditional cuisine is simple and hearty, featuring ingredients such as fish, meat, potatoes, root vegetables and berries. Here are some elements of a healthy Finnish diet:

Fish

There is an abundance of freshwater fish, such as salmon, trout and whitefish. These fish are an excellent source of omega-3 fatty acids, which are important for heart health and brain function. My favourite is smallfish smoked, hot from the smoker on rye bread with some finely chopped chives. Simple but delicious.

Berries

Finland has several wild berries to choose from, including blueberries, lingonberries and cloudberries. These berries are packed with antioxidants and other nutrients, making them a healthy addition to any diet. Foraging up your own is an exercise on its own right. And the feeling when you cook and eat them later... happiness right there.

Root vegetables

Carrots, turnips and parsnips are common in Finnish cuisine. These vegetables are high in fibre, vitamins and minerals, and can be cooked in a variety of ways. I love mine raw. Yep, just finely grated goes great as a side salad with meatballs and mashed potato.

Whole grains

Finns consume a lot of whole grains, such as rye bread, oats and barley. Whole grains are an important source of fibre and other nutrients. They can help lower the risk of heart disease, diabetes and other health problems. I love rye bread and would eat it every day if I could.

Dairy products

Dairy products, such as milk, yogurt and cheese, are a common part of the Finnish diet. From early on, you get these as part of your diet. They are rich in calcium and other nutrients, and can help maintain strong bones and teeth. In supermarkets, you have wall-high and wall-wide options from gluten-free, milk-free, plain and flavoured for every taste.

Wild game

The tradition of hunting wild game, such as reindeer, elk and moose, is strong in Finland. In autumn, it is not uncommon to see men and women with orange coats in cars getting ready for a hunt. Game is a lean meat and high in protein. It can be a healthy alternative to more fatty meats. Though you need to be part of a hunting lodge to get these meats, you might spot them in local supermarkets in Finland.

Mushrooms

Finland's forests are also full of mushrooms, which are an excellent source of vitamins, minerals and antioxidants. We add them to soups, stew and other dishes. This is the knowledge that is transferred from generation to generation. I recall going mushroom-picking with my mum and granny and them showing me what was a good edible mushroom and what was not. This is something we have done with my boys when in Finland.

Many families have their version of family favourites; classic meatballs and mashed potato is one that my kids love and a very Nordic dish to have. Check out my *Nordic Lifestyle* book for the meatball recipe that I use at home.

If you want some more Finnish recipes, I recommend looking at *Her Finland* blog by Varpu Rusila, who has everything from day-to-day dinner recipes to baking.

Overall, the Finnish diet is a great example of how healthy eating can be delicious and satisfying. I try to incorporate all these into my diet and into the food that I cook at home. When you focus on whole, natural foods that are locally sourced and seasonal, it is better for you and the environment, which is what I want to talk about next.

RIGHT *Community garden in Finland where you can grow your fruit and vegetables.*

CHAPTER 10

Sustainability is something I think about all the time. In fact, while writing this book, I started studying sustainability. It is so clear to me that Finland – along with all the other Nordic countries – is so far ahead with sustainability that it leaves the rest of the world in shame. Finland has been well and truly integrating the concept of sustainability into people's lives for a long time and well before I left Finland at the end of the 1990s. Yes, there is always more to do, but climate change data shows Finland is topping the rankings on action.

When I moved to London before the millennium, it was a rough day when I realised there were no longer four different recycling bins from the council. All the rubbish went into one bin. People did not seem to know about plastic waste and were ignorant about how it pollutes rivers and lakes, even though I recalled reading about it at school years – if not decades – before.

Since I started studying sustainability, I have thought a lot about how it relates to happiness. How does being sustainable contribute to happiness or is it the other way around? Does happiness contribute to a tendency towards sustainability?

Finland has encouraged sustainability and a circular economy, but why and how does it improve Finns' lives? Does this make us happier? Well, talking from my own perspective, don't you feel happier when you are doing something to keep nature from being polluted? Don't you prefer putting your cans, glass and other materials back into circulation rather than adding them to the landfill? Isn't it great to know that you can return cardboard and paper to the life cycle and it gets made into recycled products so fewer trees are cut down to produce more paper?

New technology is advancing, so we can now reuse more products and equipment that we once thought we would never be able to recycle. There are materials like glass, aluminium, gold, silver and copper in iPhones, iPads and computers that we used to send to the landfill. Now we have technology to rip those precious metals and reuse them. With more advanced technology, we might need less of these metals from the earth, which after all is a limited resource.

Finland has no extreme hunger or malnutrition, no extreme poverty either, because it is supported by social welfare. The country also has universal healthcare available to everyone. I could add many things to this list from the Sustainable Development Goals (SDG) index. However, in terms of climate change, Finland is well away, achieving their SDGs by 2030. Actions that Finnish companies need to take on climate change are slower than they could be. Inequality between people has also grown. Irresponsible consumption of natural resources and products has grown worldwide, many of these being imported to Finland from overseas. Biodiversity is getting worse rather than better and there are more and more species on the threatened list every year. (You can review Finland's SDGs in the reference section of this book.)

So, happiness together with sustainability leads to a happier lifestyle, and a life that is going to be happier for the long run, but does happiness contribute towards sustainable life choices? Are we more likely to make eco-friendly choices if we are happier? Well, I would like to think so, but also studies have actually shown that living sustainably can lead to better life satisfaction and overall well-being. All that I have read and researched about Finland and sustainability leads me to think that Finland is a happier place to live *because* of the sustainable focus the society has.

I came across the S*ustainable Happiness* concept in a book of the same name by sustainability and well-being expert Dr. Catherine O'Brien, in which she defines it like this: "*Happiness that contributes to individual, community, and/or global well-being without exploiting other people, the environment or future generations.*" This definition matches how I believe Finland approaches its future and how sustainability is seen there. Finland is working hard to make sure that there is a future for generations to come. Sustainable happiness is an achievable dream for everyone; if you want to make your life about eco-conscious choices, you can.

Finns see sustainability as more of an opportunity rather than a threat. Global climate change is here. It is not coming; it is already happening. Rather than seeing climate change as a threat to their existence, Finns are researching ways to move forward and tread their own path in this changing environment. How can they own the opportunities that changing climate offers? How will these changes enhance their lifestyle, society and Finland as a country? And how can they develop products and concepts that will be implemented, not just in Finland but overseas as well?

So, you see that sustainable happiness really can be achieved if we have leaders and politicians who want to preserve the world for future generations. In my studies, I have also come across a question of what a sustainable leader looks like. I answered this question when I was reading about Finland and how it is at the top of the SDG index. I realised it is not because we have outstanding leaders who have pushed their country towards the right direction but because the *people* have made the right choices; they have voted with their consumer efforts, their wallets and their votes, electing the correct people into local and national level governments.

Anyone who makes more sustainable choices in life is a sustainable leader. Finland has made it easier to make sustainable choices; hence, we have plenty of sustainable happiness to share beyond our borders. Finland is an example of how a sustainable life can be achieved and maintained in the ever-changing environment. Finland has changed for the better, being a trailblazer in efforts to do better and make more eco-conscious choices. Other countries are trying to replicate what Finland has done – and with good reason. A sustainable circular economy will be a requirement in the future, not a choice but because our existence requires it. Whatever we produce will need to be put back into the life cycle. Finns have figured this one out by recycling and reusing much of what is produced.

HINTS FOR A SUSTAINABLY HAPPY LIFE

What can you implement to have a happier outlook on life through some sustainable changes:

REMOVING PLASTIC FROM YOUR LIFE

Invest in reusable shopping bags, refillable water bottles and stainless steel or glass containers for food storage. Choose products with minimal or no plastic packaging. Where possible, opt for items made from sustainable materials like bamboo, stainless steel or glass.

REDUCING ENERGY CONSUMPTION

Start with simple changes like turning off lights when not in use, using energy-efficient appliances and unplugging devices when they're fully charged or not in use. Consider upgrading to LED bulbs, which consume significantly less energy than traditional incandescent bulbs. Additionally, encourage the use of natural light during the day to reduce reliance on artificial lighting.

ADDING MORE ORGANIC PRODUCTS TO YOUR DIET AND EVERYDAY LIFE

Incorporate organic foods into your diet to reduce exposure to pesticides and support environmentally friendly farming

practices. Besides food, explore organic options for personal care products, such as skincare, cosmetics and cleaning supplies.

CREATING GREEN SPACES IN YOUR LIFE
Introduce greenery into your surroundings by bringing indoor plants into your home or workplace. They not only enhance the aesthetics but also improve air quality and contribute to a healthier environment. Consider creating a small garden, whether indoors with potted herbs to use in cooking or outdoors if you have space.

SUPPORTING SUSTAINABLE PRODUCTS OVER MASS-PRODUCED
Prioritise products that are sustainably sourced, produced and packaged. Look for certifications indicating eco-friendly practices, such as Fair Trade, Rainforest Alliance, or USDA Organic labels. Support brands committed to ethical and environmentally responsible manufacturing processes. Consider quality over quantity and choose items that are built to last rather than disposable or short-lived products.

This concludes the positives covered in this book. In the next part, I will delve into the darker aspects of Finnish society, focusing on the negatives. Feel free to skip ahead to the end if you prefer to solely embrace the positive aspects of Finland.

PART TWO

THE NEGATIVES

So far, I have covered all the positives about Finland and how it really is the happiest country in the world, but there is the dark side, the shadow, like everything in life. I know many people would be happy to finish the book here. We have already talked about everything, right?

We have explored happiness in terms of all the positive ways we can measure the success of Finland as a 'happy' country, but it is important to me, as a Finn, to have balance, and so I must also address some of the negative things that have arisen in our society too. After all, we wouldn't be Finnish without this side to us.

It reminds me of the Japanese pottery art *kintsugi*, where you repair your pottery using gold and it becomes more than it was. Only taking the item as a whole can we truly be content with who we are. Maybe by fixing the broken pot, or the damaged parts of Finnish society that I explore next, we can create something more beautiful.

When I said in the beginning that I wanted to understand why Finland is the happiest country in the world, I also wanted to understand where the threats lie. For some, it is perhaps not the happiest country in the world. The next few chapters are about the negatives, the side we do not see in the World Happiness Report. The paradox, in other words.

This is the Finland that you do not see in your Insta feed. These are the problematic and scary questions I try to understand and answer, because if you were to visit the so-called 'happiest country in the world', you would not only see happiness. As with all things, there are the downsides, the ugly sides of society, ways we can do better. So, I explore how these negatives manifest in Finland.

The topics I cover here might be contentious. You might disagree with me or wonder why I bring up these issues. You might not want to read them and just jump straight to the end. And all that is alright.

Let me tell you why they're here though. I raise these issues, because Finland is not perfect. At least, it is not perfect for *everyone*. While many – and even the reports – say it is, we should never forget the other side of the story. As wonderful as Finland is as a place to live – and it really is a great country – there are areas I want to highlight here to shine a light on where we still have far to go in my view of happiness.

CHAPTER 11

The rise of extremism

hen I talked to Finnish people during the research for
this book, I asked about the things that stood in the
way of happiness. What issues are Finns facing that
contradict the image of Finland as a 'happy' place?

The thing that kept cropping up in conversations with
Finns was this one word: racism. It's a bold word and it can
be scary, but we can't shy away from it, even in a book about
happiness. Why? Because when we talk about happiness, it
isn't just happiness for the select few.

It should be happiness that everyone gets to experience.

In Finland, structural racism exists, even though you might
not see it on the surface. It is in subtle things that people
experience racism. For example, if your last name does not
end in '-nen', like mine does, you might find it harder in the
job market. If you do not fit into this white Caucasian mould,
your prospects of finding a job might be reduced, no matter
how good you are, how great your CV looks, what experience

you have, or how much you have worked and studied. Certain people might even struggle to get interviews because of their name, let alone what they look like.

I see conversations about Finland needing more people to come and work there, as it is a greying society. There are recruitment companies who target people like me, with a Finnish name and background, who live overseas. They try to lure us back with big bonuses and good jobs, healthcare and schooling. At the same time, there are migrants who already live in Finland. Why is the unemployment rate among them so high, if Finland has such a high need to recruit workers? I was finding it hard to understand the sudden interest in recruiting us Finns living overseas. There are people who already live in Finland, who have integrated into society and speak the language. They are there and willing to work. Why not recruit those people?

After talking with some recruiters and tuning into the conversation in Finland, I realised it is all because of unconscious bias. Unconscious bias is where ingrained beliefs are in play in decision-making, where one group is favoured or given advantage over another, without the person realising that they are promoting the interests of the people who are more like them. One way it plays out is a job market where people are available to work, but are overlooked in favour of Finns with Finnish names who are living overseas.

Back in the 2000s on one of his very first trips to Finland, I noticed unconscious bias in play when my white Caucasian husband was with me, because of his darker features, unlike the fair Finnish looks. At the time, he had a beard that he had been growing for weeks (because he did not shave during the holidays) and was very tanned. In a Finnish crowd, he looked rather 'out of place', which is a problematic point of view to begin with, but it got worse...

We were with some family having a meal and one guest asked my husband out of nowhere, "Where abouts in Afghanistan are you from?" I nearly choked on my smoked salmon. I was mortified. I could not believe what I'd just heard. My husband was trying not to laugh, but I felt ashamed about such comments because I understood the underlying connotations.

I calmly explained that my husband was from England, while picking them up on putting my husband in a certain box because of their world views. He was very polite, even saw a funny side, and continued as though nothing had happened. Afterwards, my husband told me he noticed Finns could be 'like children' – naïve and no filter – when they haven't been outside Finland. Those Finns who are less travelled or educated about the world are unfamiliar with its people and that naïvety feeds into ignorance, which feeds into unconscious bias and racism.

This person was putting my husband in a box just because of his looks, which is what some people in Finland still experience every day. This person did not even know that what they had said was anything wrong. They just thought it was a question to ask. Perhaps this was the Finnish bluntness that I have been accused myself a few times, but I would say it was something else.

After that conversation, my view of Finland and what a happy country it was to live in was tainted. Since then, every time we travel through smaller places, I have been wary of people looking at us, because we were talking English to each other and to our kids. In other words, we do not fit into the 'typical' Finnish model family.

Racism can be overt too, not only subtle. On another trip to Finland with my husband many years ago, I was walking on the streets of my old hometown Kajaani. I was showing him

places and excitedly explaining about the heritage and history of the town. We were walking down the main street, when I heard a man behind us muttering in Finnish, "Go back where you came from," the words being directed to my husband.

My husband did not realise what the man had said, so carried on as normal, but I heard it and turned around. Before I said a word, two young guys skulked away to the other side of the street, ignoring my stares when they realised I was going to confront them. I felt heartbroken. How could this beautiful town I had called home be so ugly, after all?

I explained to my husband what had happened and he told me to ignore it. However, I was so shocked about the racist intent of the remarks. I wanted to run after the men and ask why they had said what they did. My husband was not living or working in Finland; he was a tourist contributing to the economy. Did I need to justify myself and my husband? No. What happened was wrong. What they said was wrong. There is no place for this attitude in Finland, no matter who he was or why he was there.

Unfortunately, there are more examples like these, but it would not add anything to go into more hurtful stories here. Let's just say that one negative aspect of Finland is its racism.

Many people I spoke to agreed that this is one of the ugly sides of Finland. We might be the happiest country when measured on the World Happiness Report, but are these reports measuring racism and the negative impacts of it on non-white Finns? And is the World Happiness Report really complete if it ignores such a contentious issue that so many people experience? The experience I have witnessed is not isolated. There are those who have had a completely opposite, positive experience, being welcomed from the start. How can we call Finland the happiest country in the world, if that happiness isn't experienced equally?

The World Happiness Report does not measure racism, but I must point out this contentious issue because everyone should have their say. The experience I witnessed is not isolated. Many foreigners have a similar story to tell. And then there are those who have the complete opposite, a positive experience where they feel welcomed from the start.

Far-right politics

They say there are three things that you should not talk about: sex, politics and religion. However, I feel we need to talk about politics here. As it is very common – not just in Finland but most of the Nordic countries – that far-right politics are on the rise and conservative governments are in power. How does politics come into the question of happiness?

Let's take a step back to 2019 when the world was looking at Finland with interest as Sanna Marin took the helm as Prime Minister. She was a breath of fresh air in Finnish politics and was compared to Jacinda Ardern from New Zealand. Young, beautiful, able and well-educated, she was a beacon of light and hope for many during a very gloomy time: the COVID-19 pandemic and the start of the Ukraine war. Sanna Marin was successful in making people look at Finland as an example, not just topping the charts on many issues and measures but encouraging renewable energy transition, embracing a circular economy and promoting sustainable mobility.

However, her government lost the parliamentary election in 2023, as the far-right Finnish party formed a government with a national coalition party. I have to say here that I am not surprised by their win. As liked and respected as she was overseas, Marin's overall popularity was low in Finland. She had to make some pretty tough economic decisions during COVID-19 and the suffering economy was one of the main points of discontentment during the election.

What does this have to do with happiness? Well, this is the backdrop to what is happening in Finland at the moment. Many social, health and education reforms have taken place and Finland is in the process of changing how it manages its ageing society going forward. This is difficult when there will be a skills shortage of doctors, nurses and auxiliary staff, which is already being felt in regional areas, where there are fewer health services available. How can Finland be a happy country when so many basic services are not available anymore?

Is the struggling economy, coupled with an ageing population, leading to shortages in services? And are people turning to far-right populism due to their discontent? Far-right populism has raised its ugly head in Finnish society; it has been there at the centre of conversations in local pubs and other social gatherings. Does the happiness of Finns come from the fact that we have anti-immigration policies in place? Or that we want immigration only from *selected* countries, skills and backgrounds? What does that tell us about Finland as a country?

For me, Finnish society needs to express and represent all backgrounds and religions to be inclusive. I feel we have moved away from peaceful multiculturalism, where individuals were allowed to be themselves, or maybe I was just unaware of the problems people from other cultures were experiencing in Finland when I was younger. I would like to think not. I hope that somewhere there is still a Finland – changed as it is – that allows individuals to be themselves and embraces positive progress, not negative far-right policies.

Next, let's look at Finnish social welfare and how social exclusion has become an issue for Finland.

CHAPTER 12

Gaps in the safety net

Isn't happiness knowing your place in the world? Having meaning in life? Being comfortable at home? Happiness is not working and still being worried that the next bill will mean you can't afford to pay your rent.

Have I told you about my trip to see a dentist in the north of Finland while living in London? For many years, I made sure that I saw a doctor, dentist or both on all my trips back to Finland. Having my annual dentist appointment while in Finland, was my idea of holiday.

We were in the European Union so I could have seen a dentist or doctor in the UK for free under the NHS (National Health Service), but I would have had to pay to guarantee the kind of quality treatment I was used to in Finland. (The NHS can be a lottery!) In Finland, I did not have to pay to know the quality would be there, so I happily travelled back to Finland to see my doctor when required. Three hours on a plane to see a doctor? No problem.

I particularly took the doctor's appointments seriously when I was working for the NHS and saw firsthand how bad it could be. I did also see how good it could be, but it was one or the other. You either were lucky and saw a brilliant doctor or you were not lucky and had subpar service from your GP. The UK's NHS has been in crisis for as long as I can remember. When I was working there, it was easy to see why people chose to go private instead if they could afford it.

As a nurse, I did not have the need or want to use local doctors when I could use Finnish ones. I knew that the healthcare in Finland was first class and that the NHS could be hit and miss, a belief that was strengthened when a fellow nurse fell and hit her head and neck. She had symptoms and was seen at the local hospital's A&E (accident and emergency), a hospital where we all worked. She had x-rays taken and was given the all-clear, but my friend continued having headaches and neck pain. She took a flight back to Finland and got seen by her own doctor.

I still recall her telling me the story of sitting at the doctor's office back in Finland with her mother. She was waiting for the x-ray results when a nurse approached her and gently placed a neck collar on her and told her not to move. They helped her lie down, then the doctor came to tell her she had fractured her neck vertebra. Further x-rays and MRI scans later showed the fracture was not life-threatening, so she could return to work at the hospital a few weeks later. She took the x-rays and gave them to the doctor who had missed the diagnosis in the first place, as she wanted to make a point that their mistake could have been very serious. In this case, it was not, but it reminded them of what could have been.

Yet, despite quality healthcare in Finland, I am aware of hospitals closing down and services being reduced, particularly in more remote, country locations. Municipalities are tightening their belts to reduce costs, at the same time trying to keep the basic needs of the population met.

What about social services?

The Finnish social welfare system provides a range of social services, including child and family, disability and elderly care services. There is a high demand for elderly care services, but there is criticism on how this is run in Finland. Neglect of elderly patients, not enough staff and high costs of care are some of the comments you see in the *Helsingin Sanomat* newspaper headlines regularly.

I must confess – the Finnish government's income support scheme is tricky. Allow me to explain why. The authorities provide a variety of income support programmes to assist individuals and families with their essential needs, but this also provides a reason not to pursue employment! This aid can be classified as unemployment benefits, sickness benefits and housing benefits, though there are a few subsections too complicated to get into here in this book.

During my late teens and early 20s, when I was between jobs, studying and trying to find my place in the world, I was actually receiving unemployment benefits. There's no shame or humiliation here – I'm sure half of all young people hunting for a job have been in the same position at least once in Finland. Thankfully, our benevolent government has kindly handed out these benefits to help us through tough times. When studying you also get an allowance from the government. Depending on what you study, you get a different amount as a university student than if you are in a polytechnic or vocational college.

The way this becomes contentious is that these benefits are limited. They do not provide enough money for basic living expenses, even though some families depend *solely* on this income. Though this is not exclusive to Finland, it is important to mention that the welfare system is not perfect.

In some cases, it may seem there is no point in finding a job if the government pays more than an employer would at minimum wage. For others, taking a job could mean they lose some or all of their benefits and would be worse off. Why bother looking for a job when the job you can get does not pay better than the benefits you get from the government? In a sense, the system has become too efficient.

In short, for some these benefits are a necessity; others see it as an invitation to stop their job search.

The Finnish social welfare system provides a safety net for citizens and residents, and promotes social inclusion, well-being and equality. The system is funded through taxation and is considered an integral part of the Finnish welfare state. But as described, it has its flaws. If you asked a person who relies only on the Finnish government for income support, they might not be as happy as the World Happiness Report suggests.

Universal healthcare

When I first heard the term 'universal healthcare', it mystified me that you would describe the Finnish system this way. However, Bernie Sanders – an American politician and activist serving as the senior United States senator from Vermont – is fond of the 'Nordic Model' and has praised its equality many times. During a city hall meeting at Burlington in 2008, he encouraged his compatriots to study Finland as *"one of the best economic and social models in the world... In Finland, a high-quality national healthcare programme exists which provides almost-free healthcare for all — and ends up costing about half as much per capita as our system."*

The definition of 'universal healthcare' is where everyone

is entitled to basic healthcare no matter where you live or where you were born. All Finnish citizens and legal residents are entitled to funded healthcare services, and universal healthcare is a fundamental aspect of Finnish society. The Finnish healthcare system provides comprehensive and high-quality care to all, regardless of income, social status or health status.

As I said before, I took advantage of this even when living overseas. I always had a plane ticket on standby (with a flexible return date) when living in the UK, just in case I needed to get back home. Call me paranoid, but I was glad that I did!

Here you see another reason for happiness – basic needs being met by society.

What is wrong with this system then?

Healthcare services are easily accessible to all, regardless of location. There are over 200 hospitals and health centres throughout Finland, and patients can access services through either public or private providers. However, there are problems within the municipalities in terms of looking after the system.

There is a lack of specialists and tests available in some places. People need to travel to another city or municipality for testing or to even be seen or receive treatment. I recall my grandfather having to travel over three hours to a bigger hospital as the chemotherapy he required was not available in his nearest one. When you live in a scarcely populated country, this is to be expected. However, when governments have been tightening their belts because of an ever-greying society that requires more and more services, for these services to be scarcely available makes you question the level of healthcare people receive, and what is right and what is wrong. There is conversation in Finland about the current healthcare system and how it is affecting people – becoming less equitable. People in bigger cities are at an advantage more so than those living in more remote locations. Not so 'universal' healthcare anymore...

Does happiness have a price then? Is the price living in a city so that you have access to healthcare? And when you are not in a populated area, is it a less happy outcome? Many Finns might say yes. My family lives in a regional area, and though there are hospitals nearby, if cuts are done and services lost, a mere few kilometres' drive into town might become a few hours to locate the right specialist.

Social exclusion

Social exclusion is a phenomenon that occurs when individuals or groups in a society are marginalised, excluded or disadvantaged in various ways, such as through access to social, economic and political resources, services and opportunities. In Finland, social exclusion is a complex issue that affects various groups in society, including immigrants, people with disabilities, the elderly and those who are economically disadvantaged.

A key factor contributing to social exclusion in Finland is discrimination. Discrimination can occur in various forms, such as based on ethnicity, gender, sexual orientation, age and disability. Discrimination can limit access to education, employment and other opportunities, leading to social and economic exclusion.

Discrimination against Roma minorities is well-documented and discussed in Finnish media, for example. Typically, this includes harassment or refusal of services, jobs or more limited offerings to Roma people. Finland has been cautioned by the UN and other international human rights organisations about the unequal treatment of Roma people.

Immigrants are another group in Finland who are vulnerable to social exclusion. Many face language barriers, cultural differences and discrimination, which can make it difficult to access employment, education and other opportunities, as I touched on earlier. These challenges can lead to a sense of social isolation and exclusion from Finnish society.

It can be hard for a refugee to find a place in Finland, in a less populated area, even more so. However, I take heart that there are many success stories like Jade Ventoniemi, who shows her love of Finland in her Instagram feed under *@jaja.ciao* and celebrates the differences and similarities between her American culture and Finnish culture.

The elderly are also at risk of social exclusion in Finland. The population is ageing and older cohorts are growing. Older individuals often face challenges related to health, mobility and isolation, which can limit their participation in social and economic activities. At 94, my grandmother is my role model of who I want to be when I am older. Her social life is as busy as a 20-year-old. She has a vast social network and is always busy; she does not suffer social isolation. Only a few years ago, she travelled to Paris, France, with a group of friends. She is an optimistic person about life; her experiences through hardship and war have not dimmed her joy.

The Finnish government has taken steps to address social exclusion in the country, including implementing policies and programmes aimed at reducing poverty, promoting social inclusion and providing support services for marginalised groups. For example, the Finnish social welfare system provides housing help for those in need, financial support, and education and employment programmes. *Tajua Nyt* is one such pilot programme in a few municipalities, which is aimed at preventing social exclusion and providing one-on-one support for young people.

Despite these efforts, social exclusion remains a significant issue in Finland. More work needs to be done to ensure that all individuals and groups in society have access to the resources, services and opportunities they need to fully take part in social and economic life.

CHAPTER 13

Overwork and burnout

When you have to be the super parent and employee combining work and life to get everything done, there are modern expectations of you keeping it all together: parent, life and your work. Does that sound right? Can you relate to stretching yourself too thin, seeming unable to achieve your goals, and being in a circle of stress and demands? Normal life becomes unimaginably hard this way and you cannot see your way out.

When I was in a high stress corporate career in the UK many years ago, I felt like I was going through burnout. At the time, I did not call it that. But later, when I was older and had some distance from the job, I could see that I had been going through burnout for sure. I was tearful. Going to work was hard. I hated some aspects of my job, though I loved the fast pace of my work and my colleagues.

I might have been in the UK then and I might be in Australia now, but I can still relate this topic very much to

Finland. Finland has a high level of burnout, like many western countries. About a quarter of the Finnish workforce suffers from burnout and around 2–3% of these are serious cases.

They do not measure this in happiness reports or the gender equality reports that Finland also tops. The Finnish workplace can be debilitating in terms of its demands on modern society. With work-related cuts and more responsibilities required from the workforce, people are stretched thin. Also, with the ageing population, there is a shortage of skilled workforce in particular areas, which further contributes to the burnout factor.

Could Finland be happier if there were fewer demands on people from this modern way of living? I believe this is a universal question that applies to all modern countries. However, in Finland, people are very thorough at work. We love to do our work properly. Even when it is stressful, the way we approach life is the way we approach work. Get your job done, thoroughly, successfully and properly. I do not think laziness is associated with Finnish workers.

I have had a few employment opportunities because I am from Finland. I asked why I was hired for a particular role and my manager answered, "Because you are from Finland and any Finnish people I have worked with have never let me down."

Perhaps the Finnish workforce needs to do less planning and be less perfectionist in their performance, though. After all, this level of meticulousness causes time pressure and stress, which isn't conducive to happiness! Longer hours in the office and less time with family and friends being social – that's not contributing to any happiness at all.

From conversations with Finnish friends, I know a lot could be done better; the burnout factor comes from how you perceive yourself and what expectations you put onto yourself.

Can you be happy and burnt out? Well, of course you can be happy and suffer from burnout. Though burnout can lead to mental health issues if not addressed.

Burnout seems most prevalent amongst teachers, nurses and those who are in direct contact with people. My sister has talked to me about burnout among teachers who work long hours and are expected to take on more – with little financial incentive and behaviour of kids being less supportive. There are teachers who have left the workforce. This, in turn, affects the rest of the teaching staff who are left to work harder and longer to cover more hours and classes.

The World Happiness Report does not cover how burnout and its effects impact society through sick days, nor the crippling knock-on effect that has on the rest of the workforce.

However, I see it as a positive that Finnish society is talking about this, and there is lots of research being put into diagnosis of and preventative measures for burnout. People are more open about this issue than perhaps a few years ago. Many famous people have come out and explained that they suffered from burnout, which opened the conversation for people to not feel ashamed to say they are not coping with life, work and expectations.

Finland is heading towards burnout, but we expect Finland to be the happiest country in the world every year? I wonder how sustainable that is!

While we expat Finns look back at Finland and remember it as a perfect place to live, grow up and lead a wonderful life, we need to remember the reality is not all rosy. There are other issues to consider, including how our perfectionist tendencies play a part.

Mental health issues

A big part of the Finnish psyche has been that we do not want to talk and confront uncomfortable issues. For generations, there has been silence about mental health, mental trauma and post-traumatic stress, and I see a trend depending on which generation you belong to.

The mental health question is hard. I think we all know someone that suffers or has suffered mental health issues. This is no different in Finland. There are lots of support services and people are more open to talking about their mental health issues than they used to be. However, stigma is still strong in Finnish society.

> *"[There are] pretty high rates of depression and the lack of social networks and the resulting risk of social exclusion, which in turn leads to mental health problems and substance abuse."*
>
> Julia V

Why is there such a high rate of depression and other mental health issues in Finland? A complex question with a complex answer. My view is that as people talk about these issues more, they reach out for help more. With diagnosis and medical help being more readily available, more cases are diagnosed.

There is an old saying that Finns are depressed because of the darkness, the long dark days. The further north you go, the less daylight you get for part of the year. For sure, I

understand there is more seasonal affective disorder (SAD) in Finland, which is related to the change of the season. However, perhaps living in darkness most of the year has made us more resilient against getting depressed, though there is a link between depression and lack of vitamin D from the sun. Besides, isn't it true that sunshine makes us all that little bit happier? When the weather has been gloomy and dark, we get a lift from the fact that it is sunny again. Finns also tend to escape to warmer places for a few weeks to top up their batteries with sunshine during winter.

Whatever the reasons, we see more mental health issues reported amongst young children, teenagers and young adults. Again, yes, we report them more. We have systems in place to catch things like these early. However, mental health issues, particularly depression, have been linked to social media bullying and how digital devices have become escapism for many people.

Finland, like so many countries, has issues with social isolation, loneliness and lack of belonging. Limited friendship groups or social contacts might contribute to this. In addition, there is discrimination because of sexual or social stigma. For example, many minorities feel left out, discriminated against or shunned. It is well-known that this can lead to mental health issues.

I recall my university friend whose heritage was Saami from Lapland. She was a very talkative and friendly girl. However, she told me she found it difficult to make friendships with people. She always held herself back and feared letting people get too close. This was her defence mechanism due to being shunned at school because of her looks, customs and wearing her traditional *gákti*.

I could not help but wonder how we Finns still did not really understand Saami culture and customs. Even today, this is something we struggle with. The Saami people are the only indigenous people of Europe and they live in northern parts of Norway, Sweden, Finland, and on the Kola Peninsula in Russia. You can read more in my *Nordic Lifestyle* book where I talk more about the Saami people. Saami status as an indigenous people and their cultural self-government is recognised in the Finnish Constitution. However, there have been attempts to provide insight into discrimination towards Saami people and their rights to govern their land, government inclusion policies and violations of rights, but these have not succeeded due to political resistance.

Social isolation can lead to poor mental and physical health outcomes, reduced productivity and engagement in work or other activities, and a lower quality of life. In Finland, social isolation has been identified as a significant public health concern, particularly among elderly populations.

The youth of Finland are struggling too. There is an obvious need for some reforms at school, as good as they are. Students who slip between the cracks, who do not engage with learning and face learning difficulties and mental health issues have increased.

My sister Johanna Heiskanen, who I interviewed for my *Nordic Lifestyle* book, talks about burnout of kids and teachers alike. So often, the teachers are left to teach kids basic life skills like time management, coming to school and handing in exam papers on time. Why have teachers ended up with these tasks? Are parents too busy at work? I will talk more about this later in this section.

Overall, mental health issues with children have increased. There are complex issues behind why this is the case, including better detection of mental health issues amongst children, which is of course positive. Early intervention in kids is better that it was when I was young. Many school-aged children get counselling and receive the help they need, something that was not in place when I was younger. There was a less robust support network than we have now.

In children from less advantaged backgrounds, having more to worry about from an early age can be a contributing factor. Social media usage and trolling can also be detrimental for the mental health of young people when they are just learning

the ropes of life. My son won't get an account until he goes to high school. He might not like that rule, but I was trying my best to protect him and give him time to develop. He will be more mature when he gets into social media and by then should be equipped with morals, knowing right from wrong.

The older generation has their own issues in terms of not being able to talk and open up. They still harbour post-war feelings and are of that generation who had parents that were not open with their feelings or able to talk about everything with their children. This feeling of not been able to talk is then passed to the younger generation and the cycle of bad feelings can mount up as mental health issues.

I know I sound like a broken record listing all these, but Finland's mental health helpline has seen call volumes double over the past few years, COVID-19 not helping the issue.

Though the new generation is getting better at this. We do not dwell on things; we share them with friends and family and talk openly about issues. I feel that there is a need to be more open about these things. We Finns want to pretend there's 'nothing to see here', but so often these issues are hidden from view. There are many examples of older generations suffering in silence and not raising issues. As I said before, I feel this comes from the childhood trauma of war and being brought up in a strict and unloving environment.

To tackle this, there are lots of initiatives in place, such as community-based programmes that provide social support and encourage social engagement, as well as efforts to increase access to social and health services. There are also volunteer programmes where people are encouraged to contribute. Volunteering is measured on the World Happiness Report and, like I talked about earlier, this is something Finns like to do. There is support to get people volunteering and be more involved with their community.

MORKKIS (Finnish) - the regret you feel after drinking, after-the-fact embarrassment due to your drunken behavior.

CHAPTER 14

Coping Mechanisms

Lastly, I wanted to explore the drinking culture and materialism in Finland, as these detract from Finnish happiness.

I grew up in a family and household where drinking alcohol was a normal occurrence on weekends and on weekdays. Having a beer and a sauna, some family friends coming over and drinking vodka shots and us kids listening to the conversation, staying up late without understanding what was going on, this was a normal state of affairs. There were always the same faces that came around, the same rituals of having some drinks, going to the sauna, having a barbecue or some food with more drinks and more sauna and drinks until there was nothing left to drink or eat. Then the adults normally moved to another house to continue the party, or we went for a sauna party to one of the neighbouring families and their houses and the same rituals followed.

Do not get me wrong. We loved hanging out with other kids and I never felt insecure or scared about what was going on. It was just a given that alcohol was part of life.

However, when we got older, I realised the amounts of alcohol that was consumed, the people who were around and those who did not hang out with the crew anymore. And realise that this 'normal' was not the norm in every house.

As I grew up, I also noticed that women were not usually so much a part of the big drinking party. They were keeping us kids happy and engaged.

I was not even a teen when I got curious about how alcohol tasted. I tried a vodka Coke when I was around 10 when no one was looking. I did not like it. Lucky for me that my experience was negative. I tried alcohol again in my teens and it certainly became a part of my life then, but I never really liked the experience or the day-after feeling. Once I was living on my own and studying, I did party hard but was also quite happy to have one drink only, as it was expensive to drink in Finland. I danced the night away instead, going home able to do whatever I wanted the next day with no regrets.

Perhaps this was one of those reasons that my drinking habits changed over the years from being the party girl to not drinking at all. And I have been happy with no alcohol for years now.

The experience I had with alcohol and how I saw it is not unique to Finnish culture, but alcohol has always played a strong part in Finnish life and still does now. I escaped my teenage years quite unharmed by alcohol. I also saw some of my friends who could drink much more, who partied harder and still had a normal life. I also saw those who ended up having high-flying careers and would 'self-medicate' with alcohol when life got tough – easier to numb the pain with alcohol than confront their issues.

Where is the line when alcohol becomes a problem then? When you cannot recall your actions from the night before? When you pass out with no recollection of how you got home? When you can't remember where you were all night or with whom? When you start your day with a drink or need 'hair of a dog' to continue as normal?

All these are signs you should be careful and may need to seek help. I had none of these symptoms though I have witnessed friends and family members experiencing these, or worse. Some who could not put the cork back on the bottle ever, who continued to drink until they were physically sick or unable to go to school or work the next day. You can read my first drinking experience in *Nordic Lifestyle* in the chapter "Relationship with Alcohol" and how it made me decide a few years ago to go sober.

Alcohol was definitely *the* drug of my generation. Cigarettes were a thing in my youth, just like vapes are the new thing for my sons' generation.

Does alcohol detract from the happiness of Finns? For sure. And while it contributes a little happiness – in moderation – there are people who suffer from alcoholism and other related illnesses. Alcoholism contributes to social isolation, mental health illnesses, homelessness and other social problems.

Doesn't every country have these issues though? Are these unique to Finland? I would say no. Looking at this after living in a few countries around the world, I do not think Finnish drinking culture is the worst I have experienced. However, there is a correlation between trying to compensate for childhood trauma we have experienced or generational issues and alcohol being *the way* to socialise.

Alcohol leads into other areas such as drug abuse and domestic violence too. Finland and other Nordic countries have a high prevalence of intimate partner violence. There is correlation between high gender equality and high intimate partner violence, although the research is unclear why this is the case.

In today's Finland, alcohol is still strongly present. However, I would argue that it is more of a social drink and used less with the aim to get drunk – drinking wine with meals, having a conversation over a few pints of beer. No need to get off your face drunk – or *pants drunk*, as we call it – drinking on your own, wearing your pjs at home while bitching about your manager.

Materialistic gratitude

Does having a new car make you happy? What about the brand-new skirt that you bought? And the matching shoes? How about the chair that you purchased that can hardly fit into your already crowded living room? Did sitting on the chair make you any happier?

I know many people think that material purchases = happiness. But the fact is that the new shiny object does not make you happy. Quite the opposite. You can feel that it is never enough. "Why did I not buy the yellow skirt instead of the blue one?" "This chair is not as comfortable as I remember it being in the shop when I was sitting on it feeling excited that it would soon be mine."

As you can see, short-term gratification does not lead to long-term happiness. But has Finland changed? Maybe people appreciate more materialistic goods than before. I see there has been a change, particularly in the more urbanised and younger generation. There is no need to go to the summer cottage... Why would you? You have everything right here at home. People are more urbanised and used to having things around them, keeping them connected at all times, feeling left out when not connected.

Today's generation is not tapping into the freedom I feel we had in our childhood. People want to have more and more and even more of everything. And these things do not give us happiness. More so, they are making us ill. We feel less appreciative and there is a happiness disconnect.

The younger me once spend a week at my grandmother's house by the lake at Kuhmo, Finland. It had become a summer thing to spend time at her house and leave everything else behind. This is time before the internet was in every house, mobile phones or when you had to be in the know all the time.

I had a stack of books under my arm when I arrived at my gran's and used to spent a week or so reading, having walks with my granny, eating her delicious homemade biscuits and buns. A cup of coffee or tea and something sweet always followed the meals. The routine was soothing, and I felt so relaxed after these weeks away from home. I needed this time away from everything more than I realised.

So, when the younger generation now feels they are doing it tough in terms of not getting the latest gadgets or clothes, I look at them, feeling sorry for them. You really do not need all these things. They do not give you anything more than a moment of gratification. You would be better spending the time you are grasping for materialistic gratification on planning your future happiness through studies, reading or spending time with your loved ones.

It is not surprising that all Nordic countries are at the top of the World Happiness Report. Most Finns share similar values on what happiness really means to us and what is important in life. Things are not important to your overall happiness, nature and community. The people that you share your life with are.

WHAT NOT TO DO IF YOU WANT YOUR OWN ARCTIC PARADISE!

MORE AND MORE STUFF

The fewer things you have to worry about, the happier you are. When we have fewer things to clean, lose, repair and take care of, we are happier about having less. The way to get there is to change how we view happiness. That is a personal journey for us all.

ACCUMULATING MATERIAL POSSESSIONS

Happiness is not how much you earn or how big your car is or your house. Research published in the 2018 World Happiness Report suggests that people in some of the 'happiest' countries, including Finland, need significantly fewer resources to support their lives than the high-consuming 'unhappier' countries. You might live in one of the unhappier countries where *things* are branded as good and the measure of happiness is tied to what you own.

IGNORING SELF-CARE

Happiness starts with you as an individual. It is being happy with your physical, mental and emotional self. It is taking time for self-care, a run in the woods, skiing, hiking, relaxing in the sauna, knitting, reading. These are crucial to maintaining a positive outlook on life.

NEGLECTING RELATIONSHIPS

Human connections play a role in happiness. Neglecting or taking relationships for granted can lead to loneliness and dissatisfaction. Invest time and effort in nurturing meaningful connections with family, friends and your community.

DISREGARDING GRATITUDE

Forgetting to appreciate the good things in life can diminish happiness. Cultivate gratitude by acknowledging and being thankful for even the small, everyday blessings. It can shift your perspective and amplify feelings of contentment.

CHAPTER 15

Sinikka Salokorpi says in her book *Finland, "Perhaps the friendliest people in Finland live in Kainuu; they are modest and uncomplicated, but also the poorest in the country."*

I come from Kainuu and I agree we are a pretty friendly bunch – and modest too, at least most of the time. We do not take on stress in life or take it too seriously. We just want to live in peace with ourselves and neighbours – to just get on with life. Kainuu has historically been a poor area of Finland. People in Kainuu have had it tough making their living. However, they are pretty content with nature, their lifestyle and how they live their lives.

What could you learn and implement in your community or family to have a more wholesome lifestyle like this?

Living a happy life is a very personal and subjective experience, as what makes me happy may not make you happy. However, there are some general strategies I can give you to help promote happiness and well-being.

If I were to sum up my top tips on how to have a little bit of Finnish happiness in your life, I would recommend starting with these:

1. **Get out there!** Get into nature and recharge your batteries. Finns live our lives in sync with nature. We get our energy from those long winter walks or foraging berries, looking at the views of nature around them. On summer days, Finns love to unwind by the lakes, fishing and swimming. Finns see themselves as part of the circle of life, not removed from it but uniquely part of it all.

2. **Surround yourself with positive relationships:** Build strong, positive relationships with friends, family and community members, who can provide a sense of belonging and support when you need it. For me, my mum friends and friends I have known for a long time have become my moral compass when I need to ask tough questions of myself and understand which way to go.

3. **Ignore social expectations:** Live life like you want to live it, not how people around you *expect* you to live it. Remove social expectations. Ignore 'social rules'. Live your life the way you want and it will make you a happier person, for sure.

4. **Exercise gratitude:** Focusing on the positive aspects of life and expressing gratitude for them can help shift your mindset towards a happier outlook. Every

morning, I write three things I am grateful for that day. You can write down what you are grateful for each day – big, small or anything you feel at that moment.

5. **Take care of your health:** Eat a balanced diet, get regular exercise and get enough sleep. I know how hard it is with our fast pace of life, but you will be happier when you put some exercise on your schedule. Your health really is everything in life and it will make you happier when you are fit.

6. **Pursue activities that bring you joy:** Engaging in activities that you enjoy and find meaningful can provide a sense of purpose and fulfilment. It does not have to be anything too great; whatever brings you to a moment of calm, do more of that.

7. **Practice mindfulness:** Use meditation and deep breathing to bring calm to your mind. I love the deep breathing exercises I use to keep myself relaxed and happy, not just when my sons are testing my patience but when I want to centre myself in life.

8. **Connect with people**: Not just over the internet, but physically see friends in person. Make an effort to reconnect, as well as finding new friends through common interests and hobbies. Social connection will support your well-being as well. Have a cause that you care for, get involved and connect with like-minded people.

9. **Help out a friend** Give a helping hand to your neighbour or get involved with the community around you by volunteering. Finns have lots of community practices and something for everyone. If you do not have something near you, create your own! Volunteering can provide a sense of purpose too, as well as positive social connections and personal growth, all of which contribute to your overall happiness and well-being. This is one measurement on the Word Happiness Report, and as discussed earlier in the book, something we Finns do a lot.

10. **Set goals:** Working towards goals that are challenging but achievable can provide a sense of accomplishment and help to build self-esteem. I set a goal to write a book. *Bam!* Nearly done. I wanted to hike a local 40 km trail that was hard-core. I set a training schedule to do it. It took some time, but in 2022, I did this hike with friends.

11. **Learn something new:** Yes, keep your head in the game of learning. 'Lifelong learning' is not a uniquely Finnish concept, but Finns embrace it with both hands. You are never too old and it's never too late to start something new. Keeping your mind busy and learning is a pathway to finding balance in this busy world, including finding a purpose that fills up your cup every day.

Ultimately, living a happy life involves finding a balance between taking care of yourself, pursuing meaningful activities and relationships, and contributing to the well-being of others. I have always felt that being happy is the goal in life. Getting there can be prickly, but Finns have this saying about happiness:

"Kell' onni on se onnen kätkeköön."
Finnish proverb

Meaning that if you have happiness, you should hide it. Perhaps this is a reminder that Finns do not shout how happy they are at the tops of their voices. They just live a content and satisfied existence with each other.

When I think of happiness, I always come back to my grandparents. There is this black-and-white picture of them in the 1950s when they were a young, newly married couple. My grandparents are embracing each other in the picture, just looking adoringly into each other's eyes. They were obviously enjoying the moment and someone captured it for them. To me, that picture is happiness as you live it in the moment.

We all have a different path to what makes us happy. We define it differently and have different cultural practices for celebrating happiness. However, there are a few universal truths about what makes you happy when you follow your path. Practicing gratitude and mindfulness, and having positive relationships around you, will make you content in life.

It is not that Finland is a particularly happy place to live in itself or that all social services work or that you can live a safe life with your basic needs met. It is more that Finland has equipped Finns with resilience, a humble outlook and the ability to cope in the face of adversity that makes it an

Arctic Paradise. Being happy with the little things, evolving and adapting as life changes, those are the real reasons for its success and why Finland is crowned the happiest country year after year. That is why I feel Finns are universally happier than perhaps other western countries.

Finns do not need a lot to be happy. They are content with less. This is perhaps the secret. They see happiness in the small moments: having your morning coffee with workmates, telling them about the fishing trip you went on with your mates or the sauna you enjoyed over the weekend. People in Finland content themselves with what there is, not what they're missing, and have a social welfare system geared towards making sure people are cared for and have little to worry about. There is little to be unhappy about...

What about the negatives? There are still more positives than negatives in Finland and Finnish happiness means there is general satisfaction around people's well-being and how we choose to live our lives. The negatives like racism and burnout, social exclusion and healthcare gap issues are areas that Finland needs to work on so that happiness is accessible to everyone.

All in all, there is a mindset shift that needs to take place if you are to dip into the Finnish way of approaching happiness. Is Finland a happy place to live? Yes, for many. Is it happier overall than your country? Perhaps so. Even with all the social challenges, there are plenty of things that are right about the way Finns are able to be content. (Just do not mention ice hockey when Finland has lost the finals!)

Happiness can be fleeting or a longer-lasting feeling, when you make it part of how you are in the world. Happiness can be an internal or external experience. It's like plunging into icy water. It's a feeling of pleasure in what you are experiencing, not an intense feeling of ecstasy or bliss. Happiness is there in between peak moments. It is a content satisfaction with life.

I hope this book has given you a glimpse of happiness in Finland. In the end, this saying sums up what Finnish happiness is:

> **"Happiness is a place between too little and too much."**
>
> **Finnish proverb**

NORDIC LIFESTYLE

Embrace slow living, cultivate happiness and
know when to take off your shoes

What does Nordic actually mean?

Other than you are from the northern part of the Europe. No
matter which country you examine, we always come back to
the fact that the people of the Nordics have had to put up
with a lot to get to where they are today.

All the countries have things that they excel at and they
export these concepts overseas. Sustainability, Fridays For
Future and Climate Strike have become synonymous with
Greta Thunberg. When you think of the best education in
the world, you think about Finland, right? Abba or Ikea and
Sweden comes to mind. For many, Denmark = *hygge*. Norway
means snow-covered fjords for many and Iceland makes you
think of Icelandic jumpers like those in a Nordic crime drama.

But there is more to the Nordics than just the jumpers!
(No matter how cute they are.) The innovation that comes
from the Nordics is mind-boggling. So many great inventors
and current sophisticated processes are originally from the
Nordics. Many green innovations are from the Nordics, like
green energy from waves, or using sustainable and eco-friendly
fabrics made of seaweed and fish skin on clothing industry.

LEFT *Moomin Mug*

I would argue that being from the Nordics makes all the people from the Nordics feel companionship towards each other. Whenever I have been travelling and have come across people from the Nordic countries, I have felt a little pang of belonging. Like that woman I had a dinner with at a random restaurant in Ho Chi Minh City in Vietnam many years ago. We had never met before. We were both dining alone and just started talking. She was from Sweden and was backpacking. She had just come across from Cambodia and was on her way to Thailand.

We spent the evening talking about life, travel and missing home. I never saw her again, or kept in contact. This was in the time before Facebook and social media. But just talking with her, remembering home, knowing that she was feeling the same homesickness as I was, missing the same things, like the snow (it was December after all when we met) and the cold climate during the holiday season...

This meeting has not been the only one. Another time, a man was wearing a *sisu* T-shirt at the Opera Bar in Sydney. I could tell he was not a Finn from the golden tan and sun-kissed hair, but after talking with him, I discovered that his mother was a Swedish-Finn married to an Australian. He just happened to get the *sisu* T-shirt as a present and thought *sisu* was a cool word to know.

These meetings with random people have always reminded me of how far we have travelled and explored the world. But the Nordics mean more than just a connection with these five countries. The countries are tied together with economic, political and cultural concepts. When you get a new prime minister in Sweden of Finland, their first phone call or foreign trip is to the neighbouring Nordic countries.

The historical ties are strong. The leaders in each country respect and follow very similar political ideology. The Nordic

Council and relying on the help of each other in times of need are important to Nordic countries.

Nordic countries have a similar outlook on life as well. The stillness of society. The 'no-hurry' factor in life. I would argue that the slow living movement is part of who the Nordic people are. It perhaps was created and named in Italy in the 1980s, but the Nordics embody this simple living perfectly by taking it easy and cherishing the important moments in life.

Since I moved outside of Sydney to the south coast of NSW, I have really embraced slow living. Getting myself more centred in life. Taking those slow walks to taste the air. Enjoying small moments. It has taken me a while to relearn good habits, stop the busyness and always looking at the next best thing. My slow life is a work in progress. But I feel more connected to who I am now than when I first arrived in Australia many years ago.

Nordic means many things to many. For me, it means home. That distant country I still call home even after all this time abroad. All these peculiarities of my character can be traced to those early years of my life spent living in Finland. The outspoken nature, the honesty, the trustworthiness. All that is who and what I am. Nordicness cannot be removed from you. Let's explore how you can add some Nordicness to your life.

Infuse some Nordic vibes into your life by grabbing a copy of my book at *www.thenordicmumbooks.com*. Alternatively, sign up to my email list at the page to stay in the know about what I'm working on next.

Thank you. Kiitos.

This book would not have been possible without the contributions of many people. Firstly, thanks to those I talked to, interviewed, or who read a chapter or two and provided valuable feedback.

A special shoutout to the ladies in my writing group—you truly are ace! I can't wait to see what books come out next from all of you!

A heartfelt thank you to Kris Emerly, my editor, who has been my guiding light on many issues and with whom I love working.

To Bea Reis Custodio, my designer, who has worked her magic again on the cover and book design.

To Sarah Fraps for proof reading and providing feedback.

Big thanks to my friends, who patiently answered my many questions and helped me decide on preferences.

To my Beta and ARC readers, your feedback and support throughout this journey have been invaluable. This book wouldn't be here without you.

A sincere *thank you* to my readers who have followed, supported me on socials, joined my email list, and shown enthusiasm for my next book.

Lastly, I want to express gratitude to my lovely husband and kids. Without their unwavering support, I wouldn't have been able to dedicate as much time to writing over this past year.

The next book is in the making, so stay tuned for what's coming next.

Yours thoroughly, Susanna H

Resources and Readings

Websites and articles about Finland

Why Finland and Denmark are happier than the US
https://www.youtube.com/watch?v=6Pm0Mn0-jYU

Finnish Schools
https://fi.wikipedia.org/wiki/Suomi-koulu

Nordic Countries Are Better at Achieving the American Dream
https://www.cnbc.com/2020/02/04/sanna-marin-nordic-countries-best-embody-the-american-dream.html

Global Gender Gap Report 2021
https://www.weforum.org/reports/global-gender-gap-report-2021

World Happiness Report 2023
https://worldhappiness.report/ed/2023/

Freedom House 2022
https://freedomhouse.org/country/finland/freedom-world/2022

American Psychological Association
https://www.apa.org/pubs/journals/releases/bul-1316803.pdf

Sisu, the Finnish Art of Inner Strength
https://www.bbc.com/worklife/article/20180502-*sisu*-the-finnish-art-of-inner-strength

Emilia Lahti, Sisulab
https://www.sisulab.com/

Maternity Package and Baby Box Information
https://en.wikipedia.org/wiki/Maternity_package or https://en.wikipedia.org/wiki/Mannerheim_League_for_Child_Welfare

Kide Science
https://www.kidescience.com/en/

Code School
https://www.codeschool.fi/

Prof. Pasi Sahlbergh Interview With Greenmountain School
https://www.greenmountainschool.com.au/post/10-takeaways-from-our-event-with-professor-pasi-sahlberg

Sanna Marin on Finland
https://www.washingtonpost.com/business/2020/02/03/finland-american-dream/

Bernie Sanders on Finland
https://www.washingtonpost.com/world/2020/02/03/bernie-sanders-is-fan-nordic-model-finlands-leader-says-its-american-dream/

Tajua Nyt
https://www.sitra.fi/en/news/kerava-latest-pilot-project-reduce-social-exclusion/

Scottish Prime Minister on the Baby Box
https://www.gov.scot/news/celebrating-five-years-of-the-baby-box/

Baby Box Scotland
https://www.scotland.org/live-in-scotland/progressive-scotland/baby-box

Her Finland Blog Varpu Rusila
https://herfinland.com/category/food/

Climate Watch:
https://www.climatewatchdata.org/countries/FIN?end_year=2020&start_year=1990

SDG Rankings
https://dashboards.sdgindex.org/rankings

Sustainable Happiness **by Dr. Catherine O'Brien**
https://sustainablehappiness.world/

Populism in Finland
https://www.populismstudies.org/the-impact-of-the-russia-ukraine-war-on-right-wing-populism-in-finland/

Finnish Government Programme
https://valtioneuvosto.fi/en/governments/government-programme#/

Finnish Elections
https://en.wikipedia.org/wiki/2023_Finnish_parliamentary_election

Burnout Report Finland
https://www.worklifedata.fi/en/dashboards/working-life-barometer

Gender Report 2023
https://www.weforum.org/publications/global-gender-gap-report-2023/in-full/

Discrimination of Roma People:
https://yhdenvertaisuusvaltuutettu.fi/en/discrimination-faced-by-the-roma

Burnout Story
https://www.is.fi/viihde/art-2000009531269.html

Winter Darkness
https://thebarentsobserver.com/en/life-and-public/2018/12/northerners-cope-different-ways-prolonged-winter-darkness

Colonial History of Indigenous Sami in Finland
https://blogs.abo.fi/socialexclusion/2022/03/29/a-colonial-history-of-social-exclusion-of-indigenous-sami-in-finland/

Mental Health
https://mieli.fi/en/

Nordic Paradox and IPV
https://www.sciencedirect.com/science/article/pii/S027795361630140X

Five Happiness Tips
https://www.cnbc.com/2023/06/09/psychology-expert-
from-finland-the-worlds-happiest-country-shares-the-
meaning-of-life-in-5-words.html?

What is Happiness?
https://positivepsychology.com/what-is-happiness/

Other Websites

Nordic Paradox
https://quincyssential.com/the-nordic-paradox/

Depression and Social Exclusion
https://blogs.abo.fi/socialexclusion/2022/09/26/depression-
in-the-worlds-happiest-country-notions-of-social-
exclusion-in-finland/

Homelessness in Finland
https://www.theguardian.com/cities/2019/jun/03/its-a-
miracle-helsinkis-radical-solution-to-homelessness

Six Things People Do Differently in Finland
https://www.huffpost.com/entry/finland-happiest-country-
in-the-world_l_63ce9748e4b0c2b49ad6f624

Know When You Have Had Enough
https://www.nytimes.com/2023/04/01/world/europe/
finland-happiness-optimism.html

Happiness Related to Forest
https://www.uef.fi/en/article/exploring-happiness-related-
to-forest-from-the-worlds-happiest-nation

Ploggers in Finland
https://finlandtoday.fi/ploggers-have-an-eye-for-trash-the-
movement-that-combines-running-and-picking-up-litter-
arrives-in-finland/

PISA Results
https://www.oecd.org/pisa/

Sustainable Development in Finland
https://www.oph.fi/fi/koulutus-ja-tutkinnot/kestavan-kehityksen-tilanne-suomessa

Sustainable Happiness Interview
https://thegreeninterview.com/interview/educating-for-sustainable-happiness/

Quote
Kristiina Roosimaa
https://keidesign.ca/

Books about Sisu
Sisu
by Joanna Nylund

Finding Sisu, Everyday Sisu and The Finnish Way
by Katja Pantzar

Gentle Power
by Emilia Elizabeth Lahti

Sisu – Resilience Belonging Purpose
by Jesse Karjalainen

Other readings
The Book of Nordic Self-Care
by Elizabeth Carlsson

Finland
by Sinikka Salokorpi

RIGHT *Espoo*

About the Author

Susanna Heiskanen, a Finnish mother of two, resides in Australia with her husband. She is an experienced podcaster, blogger and author. *Nordic Lifestyle* marked her debut as an author, a book sharing her experiences and life in the Nordics. Her second Nordic nonfiction book, *Arctic Paradise*, delves into Finland's status as the happiest country on earth, exploring both its vibrant joy and its darker shades. When not writing, Susanna enjoys hiking, biking and climbing in the vast national parks of Australia, where she lives.

Printed in the USA
CPSIA information can be obtained
at www.ICGtesting.com
LVHW060015200424
777541LV00001B/4